A Close Look at

CLOSE READING

GRADES K–5

A Close Look at

CLOSE READING

TEACHING STUDENTS TO ANALYZE COMPLEX TEXTS | **GRADES K–5**

DIANE LAPP

BARBARA MOSS

MARIA GRANT

KELLY JOHNSON

ASCD

1703 N. Beauregard St. • Alexandria, VA 22311-1714 USA
Phone: 800-933-2723 or 703-578-9600 • Fax: 703-575-5400
Website: www.ascd.org • E-mail: member@ascd.org
Author guidelines: www.ascd.org/write

Judy Seltz, *Executive Director,* Stefani Roth, *Publisher;* Genny Ostertag, *Director, Content Acquisitions;* Julie Houtz, *Director, Book Editing & Production;* Katie Martin, *Editor;* Donald Ely, *Senior Graphic Designer;* Mike Kalyan, *Manager, Production Services;* Keith Demmons, *Desktop Publishing Specialist;* Andrea Wilson, *Production Specialist*

All material from the Common Core State Standards for English/Language Arts & Literacy in History/Social Studies, Science, and Technical Subjects © 2010 by the National Governors Association Center for Best Practices and Council of Chief State School Officers. All rights reserved.

All referenced trademarks are the property of their respective owners.

All web links in this book are correct as of the publication date below but may have become inactive or otherwise modified since that time. If you notice a deactivated or changed link, please e-mail books@ascd.org with the words "Link Update" in the subject line. In your message, please specify the link, the book title, and the page number on which the link appears.

PAPERBACK ISBN: 978-1-4166-1947-5   ASCD product #114008   n1/15
PDF E-BOOK ISBN: 978-1-4166- 2034-1; see Books in Print for other formats.

Quantity discounts: 10–49, 10%; 50+, 15%; 1,000+, special discounts (e-mail programteam@ascd.org or call 800-933-2723, ext. 5773, or 703-575-5773). For desk copies, go to www.ascd.org/deskcopy.

Library of Congress Cataloging-in-Publication Data

Lapp, Diane.
  A close look at close reading : teaching students to analyze complex texts, grades K-5 / Diane Lapp, Barbara Moss, Maria Grant, Kelly Johnson.
     pages cm
  Includes bibliographical references and index.
  ISBN 978-1-4166-1947-5
  1. Reading (Elementary) 2. Reading comprehension. 3. Language arts (Elementary) 4. English language--Composition and exercises--Study and teaching (Elementary) I. Title.
  LB1573.L29 2015
  372.4--dc23

                              2014038767

24 23 22 21 20 19 18 17 16 15   1 2 3 4 5 6 7 8 9 10 11 12

A Close Look at
CLOSE READING K-5 GRADES

INTRODUCTION

Think about yourself as a reader. How well do you read? What do you read? Why do you read? Are you equally good at reading all types of materials?

Reading proficiency is developed over time. It involves having a purpose for reading and being able to adjust reading behaviors to accomplish that purpose. Inside or outside school, people read for different reasons. Often we read for sheer entertainment. At other times, we read to deeply analyze a position statement, to identify specific information, or to compare how different authors address the same topic. We might also read a text for a combination of reasons or approach it for different purposes at different times.

As Snow (n.d), reminds us, reading comprehension is complicated and multifaceted:

> "Getting the gist" or "acquiring new knowledge" is too limited a definition of successful comprehension. In some cases, successful comprehension involves scanning quickly to find the bit of information one wants (as in using the Internet) or reading in order to apply the information immediately but then forget it (as in programming an electronic device). Surely we want to include in our thinking about comprehension the capacity to get absorbed and involved in the text (as when reading a page-turner), as well as reacting critically (as when disagreeing with an editorial). Good readers can do all of these, and can choose when each of these approaches to reading is appropriate. (para. 26)

Learning to become a skilled, purposeful reader requires the support of teachers who know how to create focused, personalized, varied, scaffolded, and motivating learning experiences (Guthrie & Wigfield, 2000; Lapp & Fisher, 2009; Marinak & Gambrell, 2008). Such teachers know when to provide direct instruction, how to guide students' developing understandings, and when to move to the side to support each student's growing independence. Their instructional approach allows students to take ownership for deciding their purpose(s) for reading and for determining if a selected text is helping them accomplish their intention.

To support the development of reading proficiency, it behooves teachers at each grade level to engage students in wide reading experiences that invite the exploration of ideas, issues, and players discussing a myriad of positions on world topics. Texts introduced for different instructional purposes should be both hard copy and digital, including books, documents, magazines, newspapers, tweets, websites, and blogs. Introducing students to a broadened perspective supports the 21st century goal of developing civic, political, financial, scientific, and literary "movers and shakers" who are equipped to make well-informed decisions about their personal and professional lives and who are also aware of how their decisions affect the broader world community. Instruction that opens students' eyes to the roles they might play in creating global collaboration involves delicately balancing attention to students' personal interests and motivators with exposure to the great literary, scientific, and historical texts we want them to know, love, and return to often for both pleasure and deepened understanding. In this text, we assert, and reassert through classroom scenarios, that this goal can be accomplished only through focused, systematic instruction from expert grade-level teachers who realize that the way to extend a student's knowledge is to first focus on what that student already knows and then motivate and challenge him or her to go further.

Although the designers of the Common Core State Standards for English Language Arts & Literacy in History/Social Studies, Science, and Technical Subjects were very clear about the delineation of each college and career readiness anchor standard across the grade levels, they did not prescribe how these standards should be taught. We can, however, infer from the early Common Core documents (National Governors Association Center for Best Practices [NGA Center] & Council of Chief State School Officers [CCSSO], 2010a) that each teacher is expected to design and implement engaging, relevant, meaningful, continuously assessed, and standards-aligned instruction. The intent of the Common Core is that all students be prepared to fully participate as learners, innovators, collaborators, and communicators in their daily lives. Later in this Introduction and throughout this text we share more explicit discussion of the Common Core's intentions, both stated and inferred from later NGA Center & CCSSO documents (Coleman & Pimentel, 2012), and some of the concerns educators have about Common Core–influenced literacy instruction

Reading to Learn Is a Lifelong Process

One means by which the Common Core addresses each student's preparation for lifelong learning success is through exposure to and close reading and analysis of a wide and increasingly complex array of informational texts. We believe this approach will be effective if it remains in the hands of skilled teachers who understand how to scaffold the instruction of complex texts in ways that support both learner engagement and comprehension. Researchers (Duke & Bennett-Armistead, 2003; Mohr, 2006; Pappas, 1993) note that, from the earliest years, many children prefer reading informational texts and that doing so prepares them to read for many purposes: to note key details, understand the nuances of carefully selected language, follow the development of ideas, infer author's perspective and implied information—all with the primary purpose of scrutinizing layers of information to arrive at a careful interpretation and evaluation of an author's message.

Students do, however, need more than just exposure to texts in order to become proficient readers; they also need the right kind of instruction from excellent teachers. Due to the outstanding work of researcher Jeanne Chall, you might be familiar with the adage that "in K–3 children are *learning to read,* and in 4–12 children are *reading to learn*" (Chall & Jacobs, 2003; Chall, Jacobs, & Baldwin, 1990); however, educators can hardly stop teaching reading after grade 3. The progression of reading skill development delineated in the Common Core standards underscores that, as students advance through the grade levels, they need systematic, focused, and purposeful instruction in order to develop and refine their analytic skills and comprehend increasingly complex texts in each content area. Richard Vacca (Moss, 2002a) cautions that the "learning to read" and "reading to learn" dichotomy is a false one, and Laura Robb (2002) points out that "what many researchers have now shown is that for all children, learning to read and reading to learn should be happening simultaneously and continuously, from preschool through middle school—and perhaps beyond" (p. 23).

Just how this delicate teaching-and-learning dance occurs as students learn to closely read a text is our focus in the pages to come.

What's Your Latest Experience with Close Reading?

What formal reading instruction did you receive after 3rd grade? For most of us, the answer is "Little." Yet we have all had the experience of sitting in a classroom and struggling to make sense of the assigned text because we didn't have the right context for learning the content or we didn't understand the language.

Teachers can and should challenge students to read increasingly complex texts, but we must remember that as students engage with texts and topics, they do so with variances in language, background knowledge, and reading skills. We must teach and support each student in both learning to read *and* reading to learn widely and deeply across grade levels.

Supporting students' close reading endeavors involves making a text's language, content, and structure increasingly accessible through purposeful repeated readings that are accompanied by text-focused conversations and questions that respond to the students' emerging thinking. These questions should push students back into the text, call their attention to additional aspects of the text's meaning and workings, and invite additional insights. Teachers who engage students in close reading instruction do so with the goal of making text analysis a habit of practice. Eventually, the students will be able to deploy the process independently whenever they need to find a way to support their comprehension.

What kind of close reading do you engage in outside of a school classroom? Maybe you're thinking about the other day, when you had to scrutinize the warning label on your new prescription medication. Or about how you pored over the assembly directions for a new piece of furniture or the Google map directions to that new restaurant. Maybe it was your close reading of the fine print on an insurance, health, or employment document or the details of a contract you had to sign. Or when you reviewed certain character descriptions in a novel to prepare for a book club discussion, took a close look at the district's new testing policy for points to raise at the faculty meeting, or read between the lines of your sister's e-mail message to try to figure out what she really hopes to get for her birthday. Diane recently had a close reading experience when she gathered with a group of friends to play Mexican Train, a game played with dominoes. As it happened, different players came in with different interpretations of the game's rules, and eventually, a copy of the official rules was downloaded and printed. For the rest of the evening, whenever a point of contention arose about proper procedure, these rules were closely read multiple times by multiple players and then collaboratively discussed before play resumed.

As Diane watched and listened, it was obvious to her that the way that the players kept returning to the game's directions (text) to scrutinize the language and the diagrams (structure) was very much like what students do as they return to a text for closer and closer analysis to find author clues and cues that help them understand what is being stated, what is being implied, and what is being left unsaid. Diane realized that she and the other players were not only closely reading the text but also closely reading the situation and one another's tone of voice, word choices, and body language in order to agree on how to proceed.

As we hope this example and your own have clarified, close reading is far from just a "school skill" to be taught and tested as part of Common Core implementation; it's a regular part of daily life. Every day, we and our students are called on to use cues and clues to arrive at reasoned interpretations of both spoken and written language, both inside the classroom and out in the world.

A Preview of the Text Ahead

The Common Core State Standards place close text reading in the spotlight as never before and give special attention to the close reading of informational text. While willing to teach students to engage in close reading of a wide array of texts, both literary (e.g., stories, poetry, drama) and informational, many educators are wondering what, exactly, this involves. Through our own teaching and conversations with our colleagues, we have arrived at one understanding of how to teach students to closely read texts, which we share with you in this publication. In the pages ahead, we use classroom scenarios to address a number of questions:

- What is the process for closely reading a text?
- Is the process of close reading similar across the grades and content areas?
- Why should students learn the process of closely reading a text?
- How can students in grades K–2 engage in closely reading a text when they can't yet read fluently?
- How does close reading align with the other classroom literacy practices— writing, speaking, and listening?
- Can close reading occur within a variety of grouping arrangements?
- How can the background knowledge and language readers need to engage with a text be "backfilled" rather than "frontloaded"?

- How can the complexity of a text be determined?
- What are text-dependent questions, and how do they support close reading?
- How often should students engage in close reading and within what contexts?
- How does formative assessment during close reading support differentiated instruction?
- What do the Common Core assessments that focus on close text reading really measure?

In **Chapter 1,** we tackle the topic of complex texts from multiple vantage points. First, we discuss the factors that make a text complex. Then we offer rubrics for evaluating the complexity of a text. Finally, we model how to use these rubrics to evaluate the complexity of both literature and informational texts. We highlight the fact that what a teacher identifies as the factors of text complexity must be addressed as explicit points of instruction. Identification of these factors depends on the characteristics of each of the students who will be reading the text as well as the features of the text. Using examples, we illustrate how both primary and intermediate grade teachers use the text complexity rubrics to identify the teaching points they will need to address if their students are to have successful close text reading experiences with both literary and informational texts. Many of the texts selected as examples are from Appendix B of the Common Core State Standards for ELA/literacy, which provides exemplars of grade-level texts.

In **Chapter 2,** we focus on the reader and how information is processed during close reading. We also look at the process of close reading and the comprehension benefits it brings. The differences between shared and close reading practice and instruction, along with ideas about how often to engage students in close reading, are also addressed.

In **Chapter 3,** we discuss the practical tasks of planning, implementing, and managing close reading instruction. Using illustrations from both primary and intermediate classrooms, we look at how to do the following:

- Identify initial teaching points for a close reading
- Create effective text-dependent questions
- Prepare a text for a close reading
- Model text annotation and close reading
- Support students as they engage in close text reading
- Revise teaching points during a close reading
- Integrate close reading as a part of the school day

- Design various grouping configurations to support close reading
- Support English language learners and striving readers
- Use sentence frames to support academic language use during close reading conversations
- Differentiate instruction and instructional supports

We have been mindful to make these composite classrooms in our scenarios diverse—reflective of today's typical school environments, where students are likely to present a variety of linguistic, cultural, and academic differences. We are also careful to show how the identified strategies can be scaffolded to support the learning of all of these children.

Chapter 4 describes disciplinary literacy and then shares why close reading should be a component of learning in each of the disciplines. Noting that texts are classified by the Common Core standards as *narrative, informational, persuasive/ argumentative,* and *additional forms,* we discuss the characteristics of each and offer justifications to clarify why there has been so much emphasis of late on reading informational texts, both in digital and print forms. We compare the Common Core's text exemplars and other texts, and we include a chart to provide an easy reference of informational texts across grade levels and disciplines. We also discuss how the development of close reading skills might progress within each discipline under the guidance of an expert teacher.

Engaging in a close reading involves communication through speaking, listening, and also writing. **Chapter 5** identifies the language, speaking and listening, and writing standards within the Common Core that support close reading experiences. We share examples of instructional routines that develop these literacies, paying special attention to the skill development associated with Writing Standard 1 (CCRA.W.1), in which students first state opinions, then support those opinions with data, and finally, by the time they arrive in 6th grade, are ready to take a stance and pose an argument. We share sentence frames that support the development of language students need to state opinions and make arguments. All of the instructional scenarios in this chapter illustrate the need to continually strengthen the language abilities of all students so they are able to engage in collaborative, student-to-student conversations about the texts they are closely reading and use the information learned from a close reading to support the stances they will later share through their written and spoken positions.

We also include self-assessment measures that enable students to evaluate their own performance as listeners and speakers.

Chapter 6 emphasizes the value of formative assessment for student learning and instructional planning, particularly when it comes to teaching students to analyze complex texts. We begin by defining and illustrating the cycle of formative assessment and sharing examples of how to collect and make instructional use of formative assessment data. Then we take a look at the Common Core assessments under development and the specific tasks that are being assessed, along with the related standards. The instructional scenarios provided illustrate how teachers can use formative assessment data gleaned during and after instruction to modify and support their close reading instruction.

Before we proceed, however, we want to take a few minutes to talk about the elephant in the room. We mean, of course, the Common Core State Standards for ELA/literacy. Their focus on literacy across the disciplines and the close reading of both literature and informational text is likely why many of you are reading this book.

Common Core State Standards: FAQs

Although the expressed intent of the Common Core is to provide a common set of state-endorsed standards and assessments that will prepare all students with the skills they will need for success in college and workplace situations, a significant number of educators are expressing skepticism about this goal and concerns about the standards, their implementation, their assessment, and the consequences of that assessment. Fresh in many of these educators' minds is No Child Left Behind, with its publicly shared data on students' year-to-year achievement on statewide assessments, mandated program improvement for schools labeled as failing, and blame assigned to teachers when students did not meet identified benchmarks.

Let's address some of these concerns by addressing a few specific and frequently asked questions about the Common Core.

1. What exactly is the intent of the Common Core State Standards?

The Common Core State Standards are a scaffolded set of skill expectations to be met by students in grades K–12. The crafters propose that acquiring the identified skills will prepare students to succeed in college and the workplace.

There is one set of standards for English language arts, which is subdivided into the four literacy areas ("strands") of reading, writing, speaking and listening, and language. A second set of standards has been developed for mathematics. The ELA standards, the focus of this text, also address the connection of the ELA *anchor standards* in the reading and writing strands to the disciplines of history/ social studies, science, and technical subjects for grades 6–12. The anchor standards for each literacy area describe the skills students should master by the time they graduate. The grade-level versions of each anchor standard chart the gradual development of these skills.

For example, Reading Anchor Standard 10 (ELA/LITERACY.CCRA.R.10) notes that students should be able to read grade-appropriate complex texts. The 1st grade version of this standard calls for students to read texts of appropriate complexity for grade 1 with prompting and support. By grades 11–12, the standard expects students to be able to read and comprehend both literary and informational texts at the grade 11–12 level of complexity. We can infer that as students move from grade 1 to grade 12, the instruction they receive should help them acquire the skills they need to read texts that are both increasingly difficult and grade-level appropriate. If students master this standard, the reasoning goes, fewer of them would need remedial college courses and more of them would be on track to graduate within a four-year time period.

The skills students need to read and understand increasingly complex literary and informational texts are addressed in Reading Anchor Standards 2–9, which cover the ability to identify key ideas and details in texts, an awareness of the craft and structures underlying texts, and the ability to compare ideas in texts and synthesize new understanding. Reading Anchor Standard 1 (ELA/LITERACY. CCRA.R.1) calls for students to closely read texts. The grade by grade variations identify the incremental development of the skill of close reading for both literature and informational text. We can infer that this process of close reading will support students' ability to gain the skills they need to read increasingly complex texts as they move toward graduation and future work situations. We must be aware that these assumptions regarding the skill development for each standard across each grade level are not based on a body of research but instead represent the shared opinions of the experts who developed the standards. This should not cause alarm, because expert opinion is exactly how the scope and sequence charts for basal readers continue to be developed. This realization should allow you, also an instructional expert, to be less confined by these progressions and instead use them as a guide for grade-level performance.

2. Who determines the instruction to achieve the Common Core standards?

Nowhere in the standards are teachers told how to accomplish the skill development trajectory illustrated in the Common Core. On the contrary, the standards document notes that

> By emphasizing required achievements, the Standards leave room for teachers, curriculum developers, and states to determine how those goals should be reached and what additional topics should be addressed. Thus, the Standards do not mandate such things as a particular writing process or the full range of metacognitive strategies that students may need to monitor and direct their thinking and learning. Teachers are thus free to provide students with whatever tools and knowledge their professional judgment and experience identify as most helpful for meeting the goals set out in the Standards. (NGA Center & CCSSO, 2010a, p. 4)

In our analysis, concerns about teachers having a mandated curriculum are unfounded at this time; however, we encourage keeping a watchful eye to be sure that the more recent publishers' criteria for the Common Core State Standards (Coleman & Pimentel, 2012) are not moving in favor of published programs and materials that skirt teacher decision making and prerogative of use, as was initially published in the standards. Comments such as "Given the focus of the Common Core Standards, publishers should be extremely sparing in offering activities that are not text based" (p. 10) cause us to be cautious about what may really occur in future instructional implementation. Since, however, we do believe that published materials are a must for busy teachers, we remain optimistic that the individual teacher will be the determiner of what, how, and with whom both published and teacher-created materials are used in the classroom.

3. What role did the federal government play in developing the Common Core?

A third concern is that the standards were federally designed and are now being foisted on states. This is a misconception. As early as 2007, governors and state school administrators meeting as the Council of Chief State School Officers (CCSSO) voiced concerns about how many students entering college needed to take remedial English and math classes and advocated that K–12 schools better prepare students in these areas. Soon the National Governors Association (NGA) and Achieve, a private consulting firm, entered the discussion, noting that a review of state standards indicated that states had different expectations regarding what should be learned in school. With better coordination, they theorized, students throughout the United States could acquire the same skills, regardless of their school location. Together, NGA and Achieve began seeking advice from education experts about what these skills should be, consulting business leaders regarding the literacy skills needed for workplace success as well as higher education experts about the real expectations for entrance to a four-year college. The Gates Foundation supplied funding to advance these conversations and the resulting standards development. The federal government was not involved in these conversations; federal law prohibits the creation of national standards and related tests.

Former teacher and *Education Week* blogger Anthony Cody noted that the Common Core standards were drafted by a group of 25 individuals from the College Board, ACT, and Achieve. University professors were the responders to the initial drafts. The development of the standards has been criticized because of the absence of teachers and parents in the early stages. This was indeed an oversight, but the process has since become more inclusive in continuing to solicit the voices of teachers and parents.

4. What role has the federal government played since the Common Core's initial planning stages?

The U.S. Department of Education offered Race to the Top funding to states with education standards it judged sufficiently rigorous to prepare students for success in college and the workplace. Many states adopted the Common Core as a way to access these funds. Although the Department of Education did not name Common Core adoption as a prerequisite for Race to the Top funding—and, in fact, did not require adoption of any specific set of standards—to some, the Race to the Top incentive smacks of government manipulation.

5. Were states required to adopt the Common Core standards?

States were not required to adopt the standards. They adopted them voluntarily.

6. Do the Common Core standards nationalize state curricula?

The standards identify goals that, if met, will ensure that students have the skills they need for academic success in grades K–12 and success in college and the workplace. Because the standards do not mandate instruction, states and teachers can decide the curriculum, texts, and instructional methods that best support students in accomplishing the standards' goals.

7. Do the Common Core ELA/literacy standards call for students to read more informational text and less literature (novels, poems, short stories, and other fiction)?

The distribution of informational and literary texts noted by the Common Core is aligned with the distribution of texts appearing in the National Assessment of Educational Progress (NAEP), which has been used for many years to assess students across the country. In 4th grade, the recommendation is that students read 50 percent literary text and 50 percent informational text. By 8th grade, the suggested distribution changes to a 45 percent literary/55 percent informational text split. By 12th grade, the suggestion is that 30 percent of reading focus on literature and 70 percent focus on informational text across the school day. What on the surface looks like a reduction in the amount of literature students will be reading actually reflects the Common Core's expanded focus on reading across the disciplines—in history/social studies, in science, and in technical subjects. The new expectation is that attention to how successfully students read informational texts should no longer be the exclusive purview of language arts teachers.

8. Will teachers need to teach to the Common Core's official assessments?

The Smarter Balanced Assessment Consortium (Smarter Balanced) and the Partnership for Assessment of Readiness for College and Careers (PARCC) are separate, state-led consortia working collaboratively to develop assessments aligned to the Common Core. Members of the consortia include educators, policymakers, researchers, and community groups. The Department of Education has provided a four-year, $175 million grant to fund the consortia. Other funding has been provided by charitable foundations.

Because the Common Core assessments will measure attainment of the skills identified by the standards, there should be a close alignment between what is taught and what is assessed. Following a spring 2013 piloting of the assessments, many educators, students, and parents responded that the draft assessments were too long and too difficult. Less than one-third of the students who were assessed scored "proficient," with only 4 percent of English language learners reaching that mark. Hopefully, Smarter Balanced and PARCC will address these concerns through revisions of the assessments as they continue to gather insights from the tryouts that occurred with more than five million students in grades 3–8 and 11, a small sample of students in grades 9 and 10, and their teachers during the spring of 2014. Many teachers and students were also surveyed regarding their impressions of the test content and testing process. Despite very few and minor glitches with technology, the testing seems to have gone quite well, and a vast majority of surveyed students liked taking the assessments on computers and iPads. As test and survey data are further analyzed, test administration manuals and items will be revised to ensure further clarity. Language supports, including interactive glossaries in multiple languages and dialects, will also be assessed for clarity. Additionally, test versions shared through Braille keyboards and sign language interpreters will be evaluated to ensure that all students have equal access to appropriate testing materials. It appears that all related assessment documents will remain responsive to information received from school personnel.

9. Will curriculum materials be aligned with the Common Core standards?

This decision is left to states and school districts. Publishing companies have always considered standards in the creation of their materials. Pearson

Foundation, which is a major publisher of K–12 education materials, and the Gates Foundation have generated a Common Core–related professional development for teachers. While many publishing companies are creating materials aligned to the Common Core, Secretary of Education Arne Duncan, speaking at a January 2014 meeting with ASCD, made it clear that the federal government would not be endorsing any set of materials. "In fact, not a word, not a single semicolon of curriculum will be created, encouraged, or prescribed by the federal government," Duncan said. "We haven't done so—and we won't be doing so, and that is how it should be" (Duncan, 2014, para. 24).

10. Will English language learners and students who struggle academically suffer because of the Common Core standards?

We believe that the Common Core will afford all students, including those who speak English as an additional language, those who have special needs, and those who are gifted, increased opportunities to acquire the language and skills needed to succeed. Like many successful intervention programs, the Common Core standards reflect high expectations for all students and identify the skill progression students need to meet these high expectations. Students grow when they are engaged in very purposeful instruction and interventions that are identified through formative assessment. Because of the Common Core standards' grade-by-grade focus on skill acquisition and development, teachers will be able to assess students' strengths and needs and target instruction accordingly. Remember, because the standards do not identify any prescriptive instruction, teachers will be able to use assessment data to design instruction that accommodates student differences.

11. Were the Common Core standards field-tested?

They were not. Education historian Diane Ravitch has argued that the Common Core standards should have been field-tested before implementation. While we agree, we see the early implementation of the standards as a "try on/try out" period. Once teachers have an opportunity to develop instruction that is supportive of implementation, there will be real data to consider. We hope these data will be analyzed and the standards will be revised as needed to support better learning outcomes. As noted earlier in this discussion, during the spring of 2014, students across the country were engaged in PARCC and Smarter Balanced field testing to establish the validity and reliability of assessment items and to determine that they were fair for administration to all students. Schools and teachers also had a chance to determine their level of readiness for implementation of aligned instruction that is scheduled to begin in the spring of 2015. As teachers consider the resulting data, they will have an opportunity to assess the standards through day-to-day implementation and continuous formative assessment. For additional information regarding the spring 2014 tryouts, visit Smarter Balanced's report at www.smarterbalanced.org/field-test.

12. What is to be gained from continuing with the implementation of the Common Core standards?

As you read the standards, ask yourself if any of these skills is one you would not want every child to possess. We believe you will agree that if every student gains proficiency with all of the skills the Common Core identifies, we will indeed have a nation of very powerful thinkers. There is nothing in the Common Core that, if accomplished, will harm students' potential for success.

In our opinion, the Common Core standards are worth a try. A nation with thinkers who exhibit the skills identified in the standards will be a nation of citizens who are able to interpret, critique, and evaluate what they hear and read, and able to compare perspectives and take a data-supported stance while creating and presenting a focused spoken or written argument. This text is designed to support you in using your skills as a teacher to give every student this opportunity.

We encourage you to continue to reflect on what you believe are the strengths and weaknesses of the Common Core standards. Your perspective will be informed by data you gather as you work with your students, and these data will guide your decisions about how best to support each student's literacy learning.

All of the instructional ideas we share in *A Close Look at Close Reading* are ones we and our colleagues in our professional learning communities use to support K–5 students' close reading of both informational and narrative text across the disciplines and grades. They reflect the solutions we have crafted in response to legitimate concerns and actual instructional challenges. The scoring rubrics, checklists, templates, guides, and forms we provide are classroom tested, and we encourage you to download copies for your own use from the ASCD website (www.ascd.org/ASCD/pdf/books/CloseReadingToolsK5.pdf). Finally, each scenario and teacher mentioned in this book is real. We may not have used their real names, but every instructional composite is based on real classroom instruction implemented by our colleagues or ourselves.

As you think about the ideas and examples we share, remember that the success of every child depends on well-prepared teachers who understand how to design literacy instruction that includes close reading, talking, and writing about texts. Remember, also, that you are one of those teachers. We hope we have supported you in giving close reading instruction a try.

Diane   Barb   Maria   Kelly

CHAPTER 1

UNDERSTANDING AND EVALUATING TEXT COMPLEXITY

In the United States today, teachers and administrators are buzzing about the Common Core State Standards, especially the English language arts requirements for text complexity and close reading. These areas represent two big shifts from present state standards documents across the country, and they require big shifts in teacher practice in terms of the texts used with students, the reading tasks assigned, and the way teachers must think about instruction.

Why the emphasis on complex text? According to the Partnership for Assessment of Readiness for College and Careers (2011), one of the assessment consortia for the Common Core State Standards,

> A significant body of research links the close reading of complex text—
> whether the student is a struggling reader or advanced—to significant
> gains in reading proficiency and finds close reading to be a key component
> of college and career readiness. (p. 7)

To create the instruction that will help each of your students achieve the goals of the Common Core standards and, in doing so, become more proficient readers and writers across the disciplines, you need both a thorough understanding of the standards and a solid grasp of the concepts and practices related to text complexity and close reading. In this chapter, we will use a question-and-answer format to explore the questions about text complexity and close reading that we are most often asked by the teachers with whom we work.

A High-Level View of Text Complexity

Take a moment to review the following list of elementary texts and put them in order from least complex (1) to most complex (6):

____ *The Very Hungry Caterpillar*
____ *Volcanoes: Nature's Incredible Fireworks*
____ *Because of Winn-Dixie*
____ *Martin's Big Words*
____ *Diary of a Wimpy Kid*
____ *Harry Potter and the Sorcerer's Stone*

What criteria did you use in your rankings? Did you think about the content and how accessible it might be to readers? Did you consider the kind of vocabulary used in these texts and their general language style? Maybe you considered the length of the text overall, how many syllables were in the longest words, the length of the sentences, and how many concepts might be bound within each sentence. And perhaps you factored in the authors' thematic purposes.

When ranking the complexity of these texts, you were thinking about **quantitative features**—ones that can be counted, like the number of syllables, and also about **qualitative features**—aspects such as the language used, the complexity of the shared ideas, and other attributes of the text, such as its structure, style, and levels of meaning. In your ranking, if you thought about how challenging the text would be for a specific reader or group of readers, you were considering a third dimension of text complexity, referred to as **reader/text factors.** All three dimensions factor in when it's time to select a text that is sufficiently complex for students to read closely.

Answers to 12 Frequently Asked Questions About Text Complexity

1. Reading Anchor Standard 10 of the Common Core standards states that students should read and comprehend complex literary and informational texts independently and proficiently. What does this mean?

Here is what the standard requires. At the 1st grade level, Reading Standard 10 asserts that *"with prompting and support,* students will read and comprehend both complex literature and informational texts" (RL.1.10, RI.1.10). In 2nd grade, students are expected to "read and comprehend complex literary and informational texts proficiently, *with scaffolding as needed at the high end of the range*" (RL.2.10, RI.2.10). From 3rd grade on, Reading Standard 10 asserts that students will "*read and comprehend complex literary and informational texts independently and proficiently* at the high end of the grade-level text complexity band" (NGA Center & CCSSO, 2010a, p. 10).

Reading Standard 10 is a critical standard in the Common Core. Its call for students to engage in the practice of closely reading increasing complex texts represents a seismic shift from past practices in literacy instruction, which, in many classrooms, tended to focus primarily on students reading grade-level texts rather than complex texts and literary texts rather than informational ones.

2. Why is it so important that every teacher be aware of Reading Anchor Standard 10's call for students to read increasingly complex texts?

All teachers need to focus on Reading Standard 10 for the following reasons:

1. The standard applies to all students in all the content areas that are covered by the ELA/literacy standards, including history/social studies, science, and technical subjects.
2. It requires that teachers in grades 2–12 assign students texts that may be more challenging than those teachers have assigned in the past. (The requirement for increased complexity applies to grades K–1 only in terms of the texts teachers read aloud.)
3. It means that teachers in all content areas in grades 2–12 will need to ensure that their students get a regular diet of complex texts.

In other words, students at all grade levels will benefit from instruction that helps build their understanding of the process of close reading and further develops the skills and stamina they will need to closely read complex texts. All teachers will need to create lessons that scaffold student understanding in ways that will allow them to read appropriately complex texts independently by the end of the school year.

3. Why do the Common Core standards call for students to read texts that are more complex?

The emphasis on increased text complexity in the Common Core can be traced to an intriguing study published by ACT (2006), the company that creates the widely used college readiness exam of the same name. This study examined 568,000 8th, 10th, and 12th graders' results on the three reading tests of the ACT and compared these scores against a benchmark level of "college readiness"—which predicted college acceptance, retention, and attainment of a 3.0 grade point average. Only 51 percent of the 12th grade students in the study met this benchmark.

The ACT researchers then took a closer look at student responses to determine what factors distinguished students who met the benchmark from those who did not. They divided the texts found on the tests into three levels (*uncomplicated, more challenging,* and *complex*) and analyzed student responses to each text type. Based on these data, ACT concluded that "students who can read complex texts are more likely to be ready for college. Those who cannot read complex texts are less likely to be ready for college" (2006, p. 11).

The texts students presently read at all grade levels are far less complex than they should be if students are to attain the literacy levels they will need for college and career success. For example, Williamson (2006) reports that the complexity level of "college and career texts," meaning the texts students typically read as part of college coursework or that are required for career success, is around a Lexile measure of 1350L (see p. 22 for more about Lexile measures). This is 130 points *higher* than the complexity level of materials presently used with high school students in grades 11 and 12, which are typically around a Lexile measure of 1220L. While student reading materials in grades 4 and up have become easier over time (Adams, 2010–2011), college texts have become more difficult (Stenner, Koons, & Swartz, 2010).

In order to close this "text complexity gap," the Common Core standards recommend students begin reading texts with higher Lexile measures in grades 2 and 3. It falls to teachers to provide the direct skill instruction and scaffolding that students need to do so. A wise teacher knows when and where to add scaffolds that support learning within each discipline and enable students to make sense of unfamiliar language, concepts, and stylistic devices used by the author; gain an understanding of text structure, purpose, and intent; and build surface or nonexistent topical knowledge. Put concisely, good instruction supports students' reading of increasingly complex texts, first by showing them how to tackle these texts and then by giving them many close reading opportunities.

4. What exactly does the term "text complexity" mean?

Text complexity refers to the *level of challenge* a text provides based on a trio of considerations: its quantitative features, its qualitative features, and reader/text factors. These considerations are detailed in the answers to Questions 5–9.

The concept of text complexity is based on the premise that students become stronger readers by reading increasingly challenging texts. Here is a simple analogy. Barb, one of the authors of this book, is a runner. She can continue to run at the same pace as she always has, which is very comfortable for her, but if she wants to run faster, she has to work at improving her speed—move out of her comfort zone and stretch herself. It will be a gradual process, requiring deliberate effort and lots of practice over a period of months (or, in her case, maybe years). In the same way, the writers of the Common Core want students to reach reading levels necessary for college and workplace success by high school graduation. To build the literacy skills identified in the Common Core State Standards, students in grades 2–12 need plenty of practice reading increasingly complex texts as they move from one grade level to the next. The writers of the Common Core reject the idea of putting students in "comfort level" instructional materials and keeping them there; instead, they challenge teachers to "ramp up" text difficulty as students move through each grade level in order to create increased challenge over time and support the continual development of literacy skill.

5. What are the quantitative features of text complexity?

Quantitative features of text complexity are the features that can be counted or quantified—sentence length, number of syllables, word length, word frequency and other features that can be calculated on the computer. Typically, these calculations generate a grade-level designation, such as "3.5" (3rd grade, fifth month).

6. What are Lexile text measures, and how do they correspond to grade-level designations?

Lexile text measures are a numeric representation of a text's readability. They have become the readability formula of choice for measuring the quantitative features of the texts recommended for use with the Common Core standards. Like other readability formulas (e.g., Accelerated Reader™ ATOS levels, the Fry Readability Formula), Lexile text measures are based on factors such as word frequency and sentence length. However, rather than rate text in terms of grade-levels, Lexiles generate a number that can range from 0L (the "L" is for "Lexile") to above 2000L. MetaMetrics, the company that created Lexile measures, also provides additional codes to clarify a text's appropriate audience. For example, texts that measure at 0L or below on the Lexile score receive a "BR" code for "beginning reader." Texts designated as "AD" ("adult directed") are those that are more appropriately read *to* a child than *by* a child. Texts coded "NC" ("nonconforming") may have higher Lexile measures than is typical for the publisher's intended audience, and those coded "HL" ("high low") have lower Lexile measures than expected for the intended audience. For information on additional Lexile codes, please see www.lexile.com.

Figure 1.1 | **The Lexile Levels of Typical Elementary Readers and Common Core "Stretch-Level" Texts**

Grade	Mid-Year Lexile Levels of Middle 50% of Students	Text Demand of Common Core Stretch-Level Texts
K	–	–
1	Up to 300 L	190L to 530L
2	140L–500L	420L to 650L
3	330L–700L	520L to 820L
4	445L–810L	740L to 940L
5	656L–910L	830L to 1010L

Source: MetaMetrics (2014a, 2014b).

There is no set correspondence between Lexile levels and grade levels; it's expected that students within a particular grade will be able to comfortably read texts that fall within a range of Lexile levels. In Figure 1.1, you can see data on the Lexile levels of the middle 50 percent of elementary readers midway through grades 1–5 juxtaposed with Lexile ranges of the texts recommended by the Common Core as challenging "stretch texts" necessary to keep students on track for mastering Reading Anchor Standard 10.

7. What are the limitations of evaluating a text by quantitative features alone?

As you are probably aware, Lexile measures can sometimes be suspect. For example, John Steinbeck's *The Grapes of Wrath* has a Lexile measure of 680L, placing it within the reading range of 4th or 5th graders. However, this book also contains weighty themes, such as the ill treatment of migrant workers, the inhumanity of groups toward one another, and the need for individual adaptability in order to survive. Although *The Grapes of Wrath* may not have complex language, it certainly has complex themes that are beyond the grasp of most 10-year-old children.

This discrepancy illustrates an important limitation of Lexile measures: They do not assess the *content* of a text. Quantitative measures of text complexity are the *least* reliable of the triad for just this reason. "Readability" measured in this way accounts for only about 50 percent of text difficulty (Shanahan, 2009). In order to get a more realistic perspective about text complexity we also need to consider a text's qualitative features and the knowledge, language, and sophistication of the students who will be reading that text.

8. What are the qualitative features of text complexity?

The qualitative features of a text are the aspects and nuances of it that can't be measured by a simple formula. They require careful content analysis by thoughtful teachers who scrutinize texts before sharing them with their students.

To further illustrate why it's impossible to determine the complexity of a text by simply counting its readability factors, imagine a 5th grader who is studying stars in science class coming across this sentence: *The sun is a ball of gas.* Although the sentence contains only seven words, all of which are one syllable, it is more complex than it seems. A child who has good decoding skills may read this sentence with fluency and expression and think she knows what it means because she also knows the definition of the nouns *ball* and *gas.* However, if pushed for an explanation, the child may have difficulty explaining the sentence. To do so requires the understanding that gases are able to generate heat and light through the process of nuclear fusion and that the spherical shape of the sun (and of other celestial objects) is the result of gravity pulling inward. To determine the true complexity of a sentence, we must also identify the related conceptual knowledge, the language demands, and the motivation a reader needs for comprehension.

When authors write, they make assumptions about the knowledge of the reader. When authors add features like examples, pictures, and descriptions, they are helping to support the reader; without these supports, the reader must have more knowledge, related language, and motivation in order to stay with the text and comprehend its meaning. The conceptually required background knowledge, motivation, and proficiency with language needed on the part of the reader to comprehend a specific text are sometimes referred to as knowledge demands.

Other qualitative dimensions of a text for a teacher to evaluate are text structure, language features, meaning, and author's purpose. To carefully analyze a text, teachers must consider the challenges of a text in view of each of these areas. Such a detailed analysis helps to flag dimensions of a text that may be challenging to students and will need to become specific teaching points during close reading lessons (see Chapter 3 for examples).

9. How do I go about analyzing the qualitative features of a text?

To determine the complexity of a text based on its qualitative features, you need to consider the students who will be reading the text and use criteria keyed to each dimension (text structure, language features, meaning, author's purpose, and knowledge demands) to analyze those areas that may interfere with students' comprehension. Both narrative text (literature) and informational text can be evaluated by looking at these dimensions (see Figures 1.2 and 1.3), but the differences in these text types' content and purposes mean you'll need to use different criteria, which we'll look at now.

Text Structure

How a text is structured or organized is the first key consideration for qualitative evaluation. Picture books with straightforward linear narrative plotlines, such as Pam Conrad's *The Tub People*, are generally easier for elementary readers to comprehend than books like Vera B. Williams's *A Chair for My Mother* that use flashbacks or flash forwards. Well-organized informational texts often have one or more expository structures, which include description, sequence, compare/contrast, cause/effect, and problem/solution. Titles like Clyde Robert Bulla's *A Tree Is a Plant*, with a single sequential structure, are less complex than a book

Figure 1.2 | **Qualitative Scoring Rubric for Narrative Text/Literature**

Dimension & Consideration	Questions	Scoring = 1 Easy or Comfortable Text	Scoring = 2 Moderate or Grade-Level Text	Scoring = 3 Challenging or Stretch Text
Text Structure: Organization	• Does the text follow a typical chronological plot pattern, or is it more elaborate and unconventional, incorporating multiple storylines, shifts in time (flashbacks, flash forwards), shifts in point of view, and other devices?	☐ The text follows a simple conventional chronological plot pattern, with few or no shifts in point of view or time; plot is highly predictable.	☐ The text organization is somewhat unconventional; may have two or more storylines and some shifts in time and point of view; plot is sometimes hard to predict.	☐ The text organization is intricate and unconventional, with multiple subplots and shifts in time and point of view; plot is unpredictable.
Notes on Organization				
Text Structure: Visual Support and Layout	• Is text placement consistent, or is there variability in placement, with multiple columns? • Are visuals compatible/consistent with the storyline?	☐ Text placement is consistent throughout the text and uses a large readable font. ☐ Illustrations directly support text content.	☐ Text placement may include columns, text interrupted by illustrations, or other variations; uses a smaller font size. ☐ Illustrations support the text directly but may include images that require synthesis of text.	☐ Text placement includes columns and many inconsistencies as well as very small font size. ☐ Few illustrations that support the text directly; most require deep analysis and synthesis.
Notes on Visual Support and Layout				

Continued ➜

Figure 1.2 | **Qualitative Scoring Rubric for Narrative Text/Literature (Con't.)**

Dimension & Consideration	Questions	Scoring = 1 Easy or Comfortable Text	Scoring = 2 Moderate or Grade-Level Text	Scoring = 3 Challenging or Stretch Text
Text Structure: Relationships Among Ideas	• Are relationships among ideas or characters obvious or fairly subtle?	☐ Relationships among ideas or characters are clear and obvious.	☐ Relationships among ideas or characters are subtle and complex.	☐ Relationships among ideas or characters are complex, are embedded, and must be inferred.
Notes on Relationships Among Ideas				
Language Features: Author's Style	• Is it easy or difficult for the reader to identify the author's style? • Is the language used simple or more intricate, with complex sentence structures and subtle figurative language?	☐ The style of the text is explicit and easy to comprehend. ☐ The language of the text is conversational and straightforward, with simple sentence structures.	☐ The style of the text combines explicit with complex meanings. ☐ The language of the text is complex, may be somewhat unfamiliar, and includes some subtle figurative or literary language and complex sentence structures.	☐ The style of the text is abstract, and the language is ambiguous and generally unfamiliar. ☐ The text includes a great deal of sophisticated figurative language (e.g., metaphors, similes, literary allusions) and complex sentences combining multiple concepts.
Notes on Author's Style				
Language Features: Vocabulary	• Are the author's word choices simple or complex? • How demanding is the vocabulary load? • Can word meanings be determined through context clues or not?	☐ Vocabulary is accessible, familiar, and can be determined through context clues.	☐ Vocabulary combines familiar terms with academic vocabulary appropriate to the grade level.	☐ Vocabulary includes extensive academic vocabulary, including many unfamiliar terms.
Notes on Vocabulary				

Meaning	• Is the text meaning simple or rich with complex ideas that must be inferred?	☐ The text contains simple ideas with one level of meaning conveyed through obvious literary devices.	☐ The text contains some complex ideas with more than one level of meaning conveyed through subtle literary devices.	☐ The text includes substantial ideas with several levels of inferred meaning conveyed through highly sophisticated literary devices.
Notes on Meaning				
Author's Purpose	• Is the author's purpose evident or implied/ambiguous?	☐ The purpose of the text is simple, clear, concrete, and easy to identify.	☐ The purpose of the text is somewhat subtle, requires interpretation, or is abstract.	☐ The purpose of the text is abstract, implicit, or ambiguous, and is revealed through the totality of the text.
Notes on Author's Purpose				
Knowledge Demands	• How much and what kinds of background knowledge are needed to comprehend this text? • Do my students have the background knowledge to comprehend this text?	☐ Experiences portrayed are common life experiences; everyday cultural or literary knowledge is required.	☐ Experiences portrayed include both common and less common experiences; some cultural, historical, or literary background knowledge is required.	☐ Experiences portrayed are unfamiliar to most readers. The text requires extensive depth of cultural, historical, or literary background knowledge.
Notes on Knowledge Demands				

Figure 1.3 | **Qualitative Scoring Rubric for Informational Text**

⬇ Download

Dimension & Consideration	Questions	Scoring = 1 Easy or Comfortable Text	Scoring = 2 Moderate or Grade-Level Text	Scoring = 3 Challenging or Stretch Text
Text Structure: Organization	• Is the pattern of the text clearly identifiable as descriptive, sequential, problem/solution, compare/contrast, or cause/effect? • Are signal words used to alert readers to these structures? • Are multiple structures used in combination?	☐ The text adheres primarily to a single expository text structure and focuses on facts.	☐ The text employs multiple expository text structures, includes facts and/or a thesis, and demonstrates characteristics common to a particular discipline.	☐ The text organization is intricate, may combine multiple structures or genres, is highly abstract, includes multiple theses, and demonstrates sophisticated organization appropriate to a particular discipline.
Notes on Organization				
Text Structure: Visual Support and Layout	• Is the text placement consistent, or is there variability in placement with multiple columns? • Are visuals essential to understanding the text without explanation? • Are visuals accompanying the text simple or complex? Do they require literal understanding or synthesis and analysis?	☐ The text placement is consistent throughout the text and uses a large readable font. ☐ Simple charts, graphs, photos, tables, and diagrams directly support the text and are easy to understand.	☐ The text placement may include columns, text interrupted by illustrations or other variations, and a smaller font size. ☐ Complex charts, graphs, photos, tables and diagrams support the text but require interpretation.	☐ The text placement includes columns and many inconsistencies, as well as very small font size. ☐ Intricate charts, graphs, photos, tables, and diagrams are not supported by the text and require inference and synthesis of information.
Notes on Visual Support and Layout				

Text Structure: Relationships Among Ideas	• Are relationships among ideas simple or challenging?	☐ Relationships among concepts, processes, or events are clear and explicitly stated.	☐ Relationships among some concepts, processes, or events may be implicit and subtle.	☐ Relationships among concepts, processes, and events are intricate, deep, and subtle.
Notes on Relationships Among Ideas				
Language Features: Author's Style	• What point of view does the author take toward the material? • Is the author's style conversational or academic and formal?	☐ The style is simple and conversational, and it may incorporate narrative elements, with simple sentences containing a few concepts.	☐ Style is objective, contains passive constructions with highly factual content, and features some nominalization and some compound or complex sentences.	☐ Style is specialized to a discipline, contains dense concepts and high nominalization, and features compound and complex sentences.
Notes on Author's Style				
Language Features: Vocabulary	• How extensive is the author's use of technical vocabulary? • Can students determine word meanings through context clues?	☐ Some vocabulary is subject-specific, but the text includes many terms familiar to students that are supported by context clues.	☐ The vocabulary is subject-specific, includes many unfamiliar terms, and provides limited support through context clues.	☐ The vocabulary is highly academic, subject-specific, demanding, nuanced, and very context dependent.
Notes on Vocabulary				

Continued →

Figure 1.3 | **Qualitative Scoring Rubric for Informational Text (Con't.)**

Dimension & Consideration	Questions	Scoring = 1 Easy or Comfortable Text	Scoring = 2 Moderate or Grade-Level Text	Scoring = 3 Challenging or Stretch Text
Meaning	• Is the amount and complexity of information conveyed through data sophisticated or not?	☐ The information is clear, and concepts are concretely explained.	☐ The information includes complex, abstract ideas and extensive details.	☐ The information is abstract, intricate, and may be highly theoretical.
Notes on Meaning				
Author's Purpose	• Is the author's purpose evident or implied/ambiguous?	☐ The purpose of the text is simple, clear, concrete, and easy to identify.	☐ The purpose of the text is somewhat subtle or abstract and requires interpretation.	☐ The purpose of the text is abstract, implicit, or ambiguous, and is revealed through the totality of the text.
Notes on Author's Purpose				
Knowledge Demands	• How much and what kinds of background knowledge are required to comprehend this text?	☐ The content addresses common information familiar to students.	☐ The content addresses somewhat technical information that requires some background knowledge to understand fully.	☐ The content is highly technical and contains specific information that requires deep background knowledge to understand fully.
Notes on Knowledge Demands				

like Isabella Hatkoff, Craig Hatkoff, and Paula Kahumbu's *Owen & Mzee: The True Story of a Remarkable Friendship*, which employs cause/effect at the beginning of the book, sequence in the middle, and compare/contrast near the end of the book (when Owen's behavior is compared to that of a hippo).

Visual support and layout are another aspect of text structure that factors into text complexity. Illustrations and visual features such as maps, graphs, charts, and diagrams can support the reader's understanding, but sophisticated visual components may also increase the text's complexity. Layout features can also affect complexity, as can the text's font and the size of the type. Straightforward text layouts are generally the easiest for students to navigate, whereas layouts where multiple columns are interrupted by visuals can be very confusing.

When analyzing a text's structure and organization, also look at the relationships among ideas. These relationships can be simple or complex, but greater complexity means greater reading challenges. In a narrative text, you might consider the relationships among characters or among plots and subplots. In an informational text, you might look instead at the complexity of relationships among main ideas, facts and details, and the concepts discussed. For example, in the Common Core 5th grade informational text exemplar[*] *Hurricanes: Earth's Mightiest Storms*, author Patricia Lauber identifies the effects of Hurricane Andrew on Everglades National Park, explains the park's recovery from previous hurricanes, and asserts that changes in the surrounding region may result in a less successful recovery from Hurricane Andrew. Throughout this section of the text, the author compares and contrasts conditions in the park, past and present, and describes the potential effect of more recent changes in water flow, plant life, animal life, and human encroachment on the park environment. The reader must recognize the complex relationships among these ideas in order to accurately comprehend the author's message about how this hurricane has affected the region.

Language Features

Language features, such as writing style and vocabulary, are the second important dimension of qualitative text complexity to consider. In a narrative text, the author's use of descriptive language and metaphors, similes, onomatopoeia, and other devices can make it difficult for students to understand the text's meaning. With informational text, the more conversational the author's style, the easier the text is for students to comprehend. This conversational style is one of the many strengths of Joy Hakim's *A History of US* series and a characteristic that

---

[*] For a discussion of the Common Core's text exemplars, please see p. 114.

distinguishes it from most textbooks. Here is how the author introduces a discussion of schools in the 19th century: "Remember, when you read history you need to put yourself in a time capsule and zoom back and try to think as people did then. If you do, you will find that America's citizens thought the United States was the most exciting, progressive place in the whole world" (Hakim, 2007, p. 120). One caution is in order here: While conversational informational texts like this are notable for their accessibility, students also need experiences with the more formal style of textbooks.

Consider the role of vocabulary in these two sentences:

> The man walked down the street, catching the eye of every girl he passed.
> The rakish young man sauntered down the boulevard, catching the eye of
> every young belle he encountered.

Clearly, the second sentence creates a different mood than the first sentence, but it also poses the challenge of more unfamiliar, somewhat archaic vocabulary. It is precisely these interesting word choices that make the text more complex, yet, at the same time, they create the rich mental pictures we experience when we read. Vocabulary is an important determiner of text complexity both in narrative and informational texts, and unfamiliar vocabulary poses even more challenge when context clues are lacking.

Vocabulary often poses particular challenges for students who are learning English as an additional language and students with identified reading or learning disabilities. Like every other child in your classroom, they will need their reading experience scaffolded in ways that support their learning.

Meaning

The meaning of a text—the sophistication of its ideas—is a third dimension of qualitative text complexity to factor into your evaluation. Is the book simple and one-dimensional, or are multiple layers of meaning present? For example, on one level, George Orwell's *Animal Farm* is a book about talking animals, but the author's allegorical message about a society gone wrong goes much deeper than that. It is important to have identified various levels of meaning before sharing a text with students so that your text-dependent questions can prompt students to look more deeply at the text meaning with each rereading.

Author's Purpose

The author's purpose is the fourth qualitative dimension to consider. The book *Should There Be Zoos? A Persuasive Text,* by Tony Stead, provides an excellent introduction to persuasive writing that includes arguments written by elementary school children. The author explains in the introduction that the purpose of the text is to present opinions supported by facts on two sides of the question "Should animals be kept in zoos?" This author's purpose is clearly stated, but in many cases, it's up to the reader to infer what the author sets out to do. In *Everglades,* author Jean Craighead George never directly states her purpose but uses a narrative format to persuade the reader of the need to preserve the fragile ecosystem of this region. This inferred purpose creates a greater challenge for readers and, in turn, makes for greater text complexity. (Note: *Everglades* would make a great comparison text for the discussion of the Everglades and hurricanes mentioned on page 31.)

Knowledge Demands

The fifth and final consideration for qualitative evaluation is the required background knowledge needed to navigate a text, which we mentioned earlier in the example about the sun as a ball of gas. Some books require students to know a lot about science, history, culture, or particular regions, while others are less background dependent. For example, students who know something about life during the Great Depression will certainly appreciate Christopher Paul Curtis's *Bud, Not Buddy* more than students who lack that knowledge, as this book includes many references to details of the time period, including Depression-era jazz, Buddy's experiences in Hooverville, and gangsters like Pretty Boy Floyd. Conversely, students don't need to know much about the Southern setting of Kate DiCamillo's *Because of Winn-Dixie* to comprehend the story she is telling.

10. How do I evaluate the qualitative dimensions of text?

The rubrics presented in Figures 1.2 and 1.3 provide questions you can ask yourself about each of the qualitative dimensions we've covered. The criteria for each dimension for narrative texts/literature (Figure 1.2) and informational texts (Figure 1.3) will help you determine whether to rate reading material as easy, moderately difficult, or challenging for students at a particular grade level. Remember, this evaluative process is important because it allows you to identify potential teaching points in relationship to each text and your particular group of students.

In Figure 1.4, we share how this rubric was used by 2nd grade teacher Alison Zamarelli to identify teaching points when introducing her students to *The Fire Cat* by Esther Averill. With her students in mind, she was able to identify areas of the story that might cause them difficulty and then use this information to plan instruction that would effectively support their learning. The "checked" areas identify the possible points of struggle for her students, and you can see Ms. Zamarelli's notes about how she plans to address these areas in her instruction.

As we can see from her annotated rubric, Ms. Zamarelli's 2nd grade students may not need much support in building background knowledge about firefighters and firehouses. Additionally, she's confident that the text structure, style and language, and vocabulary will be comfortable for them. The teacher will focus her close reading lessons around supporting students' understanding of characters' relationships, exploring the richness of the levels of meanings, examining visual supports, and discerning the author's purpose. The text-dependent questions she plans to ask in these four areas redirect students back to the text to uncover a deeper understanding of the story.

The next example, in Figure 1.5, illustrates how 4th grade teacher David Flynn assessed the "Living Fences" section of Erinn Banting's informational text *England: The Land* with his students in mind.

Mr. Flynn's annotated rubric shows that he did not believe his students would struggle with the relationships, richness, structure, or visual supports in this text, but he did feel they would need support with the style and language, vocabulary, and author's purpose. This text is rich with subject-specific words (*hedgerows, spiny plants*) and multiple-meaning phrases (*gained control*) that he would need to help them uncover through text-dependent questions and multiple readings of the two-paragraph text. Transition words, such as *in contrast, however,* and *unlike,* are missing from this text, so students might need help understanding the author's purpose, which was to compare living fences from the past to the present day. Mr. Flynn might make the comparison more explicit by making it the focus of the lesson.

Figure 1.4 | **Qualitative Scoring Rubric for Narrative Text/Literature Applied to Averill's *The Fire Cat***

Dimension & Consideration	Questions	Scoring = 1 Easy or Comfortable Text	Scoring = 2 Moderate or Grade-Level Text	Scoring = 3 Challenging or Stretch Text
Text Structure: Organization	• Does the text follow a typical chronological plot pattern, or is it more elaborate and unconventional, incorporating multiple storylines, shifts in time (flashbacks, flash forwards), shifts in point of view, and other devices?	☑ The text follows a simple conventional chronological plot pattern, with few or no shifts in point of view or time; plot is highly predictable.	☐ The text organization is somewhat unconventional; may have two or more storylines and some shifts in time and point of view; plot is sometimes hard to predict.	☐ The text organization is intricate and unconventional, with multiple subplots and shifts in time and point of view; plot is unpredictable.
Notes on Organization		*The structure is conventional and predictable and poses no challenges for students.*		
Text Structure: Visual Support and Layout	• Is text placement consistent, or is there variability in placement, with multiple columns? • Are visuals compatible/consistent with the storyline?	☐ Text placement is consistent throughout the text and uses a large readable font. ☐ Illustrations directly support text content.	☑ Text placement may include columns, text interrupted by illustrations, or other variations; uses a smaller font size. ☐ Illustrations support the text directly but may include images that require synthesis of text.	☐ Text placement includes columns and many inconsistencies as well as very small font size. ☐ Few illustrations that support the text directly; most require deep analysis and synthesis.
Notes on Visual Support and Layout			*Words in all capital letters (BUMP! F) might be a challenge.*	

Continued →

Figure 1.4 | Qualitative Scoring Rubric for Narrative Text/Literature Applied to Averill's *The Fire Cat* (Con't.)

Dimension & Consideration	Questions	Scoring = 1 Easy or Comfortable Text	Scoring = 2 Moderate or Grade-Level Text	Scoring = 3 Challenging or Stretch Text
Text Structure: Relationships Among Ideas	• Are relationships among ideas or characters obvious or fairly subtle?	☑ Relationships among ideas or characters are clear and obvious.	☑ Relationships among ideas or characters are subtle and complex.	☐ Relationships among ideas or characters are complex, are embedded, and must be inferred.
Notes on Relationships Among Ideas		*Students are familiar with the experiences of firefighters (sliding down a pole, riding in a truck, putting out fires.)*	*They may not understand why the fire chief continues to "not say anything," implying how he has doubts about the cat's abilities and loyalties.*	
Language Features: Author's Style	• Is it easy or difficult for the reader to identify the author's style? • Is the language used simple or more intricate, with complex sentence structures and subtle figurative language?	☑ The style of the text is explicit and easy to comprehend. ☑ The language of the text is conversational and straightforward, with simple sentence structures.	☐ The style of the text combines explicit with complex meanings. ☐ The language of the text is complex, may be somewhat unfamiliar, and includes some subtle figurative or literary language and complex sentence structures.	☐ The style of the text is abstract, and the language is ambiguous and generally unfamiliar. ☐ The text includes a great deal of sophisticated figurative language (e.g., metaphors, similes, literary allusions) and complex sentences combining multiple concepts.
Notes on Author's Style		*Style of text is easy to comprehend, with simple sentence structure.*		
Language Features: Vocabulary	• Are the author's word choices simple or complex? • How demanding is the vocabulary load? • Can word meanings be determined through context clues or not?	☑ Vocabulary is accessible, familiar, and can be determined through context clues.	☐ Vocabulary combines familiar terms with academic vocabulary appropriate to the grade level.	☐ Vocabulary includes extensive academic vocabulary, including many unfamiliar terms.

Notes on Vocabulary	Vocabulary is familiar and words can be determined through context clues (The pole was the fastest way to get to their truck.)			
Language Features: Meaning	• Is the text meaning simple or rich with complex ideas that must be inferred?	☐ The text contains simple ideas with one level of meaning conveyed through obvious literary devices.	☑ The text contains some complex ideas with more than one level of meaning conveyed through subtle literary devices.	☐ The text includes substantial ideas with several levels of inferred meaning conveyed through highly sophisticated literary devices.
Notes on Meaning			Students may focus on this as a story about a cat and not understand that it is about second chances and friendships.	
Author's Purpose	• Is the author's purpose evident or implied/ambiguous?	☐ The purpose of the text is simple, clear, concrete, and easy to identify.	☑ The purpose of the text is somewhat subtle, requires interpretation, or is abstract.	☐ The purpose of the text is abstract, implicit, or ambiguous, and is revealed through the totality of the text.
Notes on Author's Purpose			Purpose is to tell a story about relationships and dynamic characters— not simply tell about a cat at a firehouse.	
Knowledge Demands	• How much and what kinds of background knowledge are needed to comprehend this text? • Do my students have the background knowledge to comprehend this text?	☑ Experiences portrayed are common life experiences; everyday cultural or literary knowledge is required.	☐ Experiences portrayed include both common and less common experiences; some cultural, historical, or literary background knowledge is required.	☐ Experiences portrayed are unfamiliar to most readers. The text requires extensive depth of cultural, historical, or literary background knowledge.
Notes on Knowledge Demands	My students have the background knowledge and will understand the common experiences in this text.			

Figure 1.5 | Qualitative Scoring Rubric for Informational Text Applied to Banting's "Living Fences"

Consideration & Dimension	Questions	Scoring = 1 Easy or Comfortable Text	Scoring = 2 Moderate or Grade-Level Text	Scoring = 3 Challenging or Stretch Text
Text Structure: Organization	• Is the pattern of the text clearly identifiable as descriptive, sequential, problem/solution, compare/contrast, or cause/effect? • Are signal words used to alert readers to these structures? • Are multiple structures used in combination?	☑ The text adheres primarily to a single expository text structure and focuses on facts.	☐ The text employs multiple expository text structures, includes facts and/or a thesis, and demonstrates characteristics common to a particular discipline.	☐ The text organization is intricate, may combine multiple structures or genres, is highly abstract, includes multiple theses, and demonstrates sophisticated organization appropriate to a particular discipline.
Notes on Organization		*Single expository text structure with facts and information.*		
Text Structure: Visual Support and Layout	• Is the text placement consistent, or is there variability in placement with multiple columns? • Are visuals essential to understanding the text without explanation? • Are visuals accompanying the text simple or complex? Do they require literal understanding or synthesis and analysis?	☑ The text placement is consistent throughout the text and uses a large regable font. ☑ Simple charts, graphs, photos, tables, and diagrams directly support the text and are easy to understand.	☐ The text placement may include columns, text interrupted by illustrations or other variations, and a smaller font size. ☐ Complex charts, graphs, photos, tables and diagrams support the text but require interpretation.	☐ The text placement includes columns and many inconsistencies, as well as very small font size. ☐ Intricate charts, graphs, photos, tables, and diagrams are not supported by the text and require inference and synthesis of information.
Notes on Visual Support and Layout		*Comfortable visual supports and layout for students. Easy to understand.*		

Language Features: Relationships Among Ideas	• Are relationships among ideas simple or challenging?	☑ Relationships among concepts, processes, or events are clear and explicitly stated.	☐ Relationships among some concepts, processes, or events may be implicit and subtle.	☐ Relationships among concepts, processes, and events are intricate, deep, and subtle.
Notes on Relationships Among Ideas		*Concepts of living fences are clear and explicit.*		
Language Features: Author's Style	• What point of view does the author take toward the material? • Is the author's style conversational or academic and formal?	☐ The style is simple and conversational, and it may incorporate narrative elements, with simple sentences containing a few concepts.	☑ Style is objective, featuring passive constructions, highly factual content, some nominalization, and compound or complex sentences.	☐ Style is specialized to a discipline, contains dense concepts and high nominalization, and features compound and complex sentences.
Notes on Author's Style			*Compound sentences are used, with several uses of commas, separating and connecting ideas.*	
Language Features: Vocabulary	• How extensive is the author's use of technical vocabulary? • Can students determine word meanings through context clues?	☐ Some vocabulary is subject-specific, but the text includes many terms familiar to students that are supported by context clues.	☑ The vocabulary is subject-specific, includes many unfamiliar terms, and provides limited support through context clues.	☐ The vocabulary is highly academic, subject-specific, demanding, nuanced, and very context dependent.
Notes on Vocabulary			*There are some context clues (dead hedgerows), but subject-specific vocabulary is challenging.*	

Continued →

Figure 1.5 | **Qualitative Scoring Rubric for Informational Text Applied to Banting's "Living Fences" (Con't.)**

Consideration & Dimension	Questions	Scoring = 1 Easy or Comfortable Text	Scoring = 2 Moderate or Grade-Level Text	Scoring = 3 Challenging or Stretch Text
Meaning	• Is the amount and complexity of information conveyed through data sophisticated or not?	☑ The information is clear, and concepts are concretely explained.	☐ The information includes complex, abstract ideas and extensive details.	☐ The information is abstract, intricate, and may be highly theoretical.
Notes on Meaning		*Students won't struggle with the clear meaning of living fences. The use of living fences in 410 AD. and the current fight to help save them is very explicitly explained.*		
Author's Purpose	• Is the author's purpose evident or implied/ambiguous?	☑ The purpose of the text is simple, clear, concrete, and easy to identify.	☐ The purpose of the text is somewhat subtle or abstract and requires interpretation.	☐ The purpose of the text is abstract, implicit, or ambiguous, and is revealed through the totality of the text.
Notes on Author's Purpose		*The purpose (to explain living fences and compare them to the present) is easy to identify.*		
Knowledge Demands	• How much and what kinds of background knowledge are required to comprehend this text?	☐ The content addresses common information familiar to students.	☑ The content addresses somewhat technical information that requires some background knowledge to understand fully.	☐ The content is highly technical and contains specific information that requires deep background knowledge to understand fully.
Notes on Knowledge Demands			*Students aren't likely to be familiar with the history of England in 410 AD.*	

By considering each of the qualitative criteria, teachers become more sensitive to the challenges of a text in terms of each dimension and are therefore better prepared to effectively instruct students as they encounter these challenging texts. No text evaluation is complete, however, without considering the reader and the task, which is the topic of the next question.

11. What are the reader/task factors of text complexity?

The third leg of the text complexity triad shifts the emphasis from the text itself to reflections about students and their levels of preparation for tackling both the target text and the assigned learning tasks. Students are at the center of the instructional enterprise, and this is as true with close reading of complex texts as with any other learning experience. According to Wessling, Lillge, and VanKooten (2011), "foregrounding student learning needs, abilities and interests provides a useful lens and necessary lens through which to interpret and implement the [Common Core standards]" (p. 92). In other words, we cannot consider text complexity without careful and deliberate consideration of our students and their strengths and needs along with the demands of the tasks we give them.

Complex texts and the demands of close reading require students to read in ways that may be somewhat unfamiliar to them. Many are accustomed to reading quickly and skimming and scanning texts in ways that may cause them to miss important information. As Bauerline (2011) observes, "complex texts require a slower labor. Readers can't proceed to the next paragraph without getting the previous one, they can't glide over unfamiliar words and phrases, and they can't forget what they read four pages earlier. They must double back, discern ambiguities, follow tricky transitions . . . and acquire the knack of slow linear reading" (p. 28). Developing these habits of practice requires time, experience, and effective teacher scaffolding.

Every day, as teachers plan lessons, they consider their readers in relationship to the challenges of a text and consider if and how they will scaffold their instruction to create the optimum match between reader, text, and task. There are four general areas of consideration that are essential to student success with close reading of complex texts: (1) reading and cognitive skills, (2) prior knowledge and experience, (3) motivation and engagement, and (4) specific task concerns. A checklist like the one in Figure 1.6 can help you evaluate your students'

Figure 1.6 | **Comprehension Checklist**   ⬇ Download

Reading and Cognitive Skills

☐ Do my students have the literal and critical comprehension skills to understand this text? If not, how will I scaffold the information?

☐ Will my students have the ability to infer the deeper meanings of the text rather than just achieve literal understanding? If not, what experiences will ready them for this?

☐ Will this text promote the development of critical thinking skills in my students?

What are my next instructional steps to support my students having a context for successfully reading the selected text?

Prior Knowledge and Experience

☐ Will my students grasp the purpose for reading the text?

☐ Do my students have the prior knowledge and academic vocabulary required for navigating this text?

☐ Are my students familiar with this particular genre and its characteristics?

☐ Do my students have the maturity level required to address the text content?

What are my next instructional steps to support my students having a context for successfully reading the selected text?

Motivation and Engagement

☐ Will my students be motivated to read this text based on its content and writing style?

☐ Do my students have the reading stamina to stick with this text with my support?

What are my next instructional steps to support my students having a context for successfully reading the selected text?

Task Concerns

☐ What is the level of difficulty of the task associated with this text?

☐ How much experience do my students have with this type of task?

☐ Have I created a moderately difficult task if the text is very challenging and/or created a more challenging task for an easier text?

What are my next instructional steps to support my students having a context for successfully reading the selected text?

readiness for a particular text. Let's walk through this process, referring to our earlier example of *The Fire Cat.*

Reading and cognitive skills. Students may have the literal comprehension skills to understand how the cat turns "good" by learning to slide down the fire pole and sit up straight in the fire truck. This is conveyed very clearly in the text and through the illustrations. However, a teacher may need to scaffold some of the deeper-level thinking skills that students may not have fully developed by comparing the fire chief to adults in their lives. Since students will most likely gloss over this character trait or not know how to understand the author's characterization of the fire chief as silent and aloof, this should be a focal point for this lesson.

Prior knowledge and experience. *The Fire Cat* is a storybook—a genre students are likely to be familiar with—and it has a clear story structure. Most students will also have sufficient prior knowledge about cats, firefighters, and fire stations. However, a teacher should carefully consider the specific group of students and how well they will be able to determine that in addition to telling a story about cats, the author's purpose includes communicating the theme of friendship and loyalty.

Motivation and engagement. It is likely that students will have the motivation and engagement to read this text—if only to find out what happens to the cat and how he becomes a member of the firefighting team. When it comes to a close reading of this text, the teacher will probably focus attention on supporting students in other ways.

Task concerns. Say the task is for students to retell the story of *The Fire Cat.* It's unlikely that asking students to read through this text on their own will be enough to support all students' success with this task. However, if the teacher provides a graphic organizer that the students can use for recording details and ideas about the story while they read, the task becomes infinitely more supportive.

For an example of how a teacher might examine the reader/task considerations with an informational text, we'll turn our attention back to "Living Fences" from Erinn Banting's *England: The Land.*

Reading and cognitive skills. There are not too many words that students would have a hard time decoding in this text. As mentioned earlier, the vocabulary might give some students problems, but most 4th and 5th grade students would not struggle with the cognitive demands of this text.

Prior knowledge and experience. The biggest concern might be students' lack of familiarity with why the living fences were first constructed by the Anglo-Saxons in England around 410 AD. Students may well need a bit more context about this time period to get a deeper understanding of the hedges with "spiny plants."

Motivation and engagement. Similarly, students without a great deal of prior knowledge about this time period might not approach the text with much curiosity or eagerness. A teacher who understands the connection between prior knowledge and motivation might give students a bit of context to pique their interest and help them engage with the text.

Task concerns. Say the task is for students to identify how the composition of the living fences has changed over time. It's unlikely that asking students to independently read this informational text will be enough to support all students' success with this task. However, if the teacher provides a chronological graphic organizer that the students can use to record this sequence of change while reading, the task becomes more approachable.

Without careful consideration of the students themselves, assigning a text like "Living Fences" could result in disengaged readers who check out in class and miss out on understanding living fences' connection to history.

12. How do I evaluate a text on all three dimensions of complexity?

For quantitative factors, we recommend using Lexile measures; for qualitative measures, the scoring rubrics in Figures 1.2 and 1.3; and for reader/task considerations, the checklist in Figure 1.6. Remember, all three dimensions of text complexity work in concert with the others. Considering only Lexile measures or only qualitative criteria, for example, will give you an incomplete picture of the text; you must also think about issues related to student needs and the tasks you might assign. The information you gain from analyzing these three dimensions will help you identify and prioritize the features you will address in class so that your students will be able to comprehend their reading.

We hope that this chapter has answered many of your questions about text complexity, text evaluation, text selection, and how to identify related teaching points for close reading. In Chapters 2 and 3, we will discuss, through examples, how to make close reading a part of classroom practice. Understanding text complexity and close reading are major steps on the journey to achieving the major goal of the Common Core State Standards: for every student to become an expert, purposeful reader of increasingly complex texts.

CHAPTER 2

UNDERSTANDING THE ROLE OF THE CLOSE READER

There's been so much conversation about the importance of students' closely reading texts that teachers may wonder if this practice involves just stepping aside and inviting students to read texts independently. While this is the eventual goal, close reading is a process, and it is highly unlikely that most students would know how to read and think deeply about a complex text if they had never been taught the process of doing so. To share expectations for close reading and to build a common language for discussing a close text reading with students, teachers will first need to model and discuss this process several times, using a wide array of texts selected for many purposes.

The amount of instruction and modeling provided by the teacher for close reading will be dependent on the knowledge students have about the process. If they arrive in your classroom with a grasp of how to read closely, obviously you will have to do less. Once students know how to read a text and think deeply about it, they will be better able to do so independently. However, they will still need careful monitoring to determine how well they are comprehending the information they are reading and how successfully they are applying the skills associated with careful, close, rigorous, analytic reading.

In this chapter we address several questions regarding close reading and explore what it means for a reader to "read closely."

Making Sense of Close Reading: Six Key Questions

1. What is close reading?

Being a successful reader means being able to uncover the deeper meaning of a complex text through continued analysis, or, to borrow the language of Common Core Reading Anchor Standard 1 (CCRA.R.1), to be able *to determine what the text says explicitly, make logical inferences from it, and cite specific textual evidence when writing or speaking to support conclusions drawn from the text.* Close reading is a particular way of approaching a text in order to uncover, engage with, and understand the information and ideas it contains. It focuses students on

- *Detecting* the overall gist or meaning of the passage by thinking about major ideas; real or implied conflicts; the general sequence of events or information; the story arc; and stated or implied philosophies, claims, and evidence.
- *Authenticating* assumptions and interpretations by identifying and evaluating the credibility the author has to write the text; analyzing the author's language (words, tone, expressions, metaphors, etc.), style, structures used to share the information, and implications; and understanding how the author used language to promote the topics being addressed.
- *Determining* how the selected passage, whether a chapter from a textbook, a description of a character in a novel or story, an hypothesis of an experiment, or the presuppositions in a primary document, fits into the whole text.
- *Evaluating* the relevancy and veracity of the passage by comparing it to ideas throughout the whole text and to other topically related information.
- *Arguing* a position or stance from a base of documentable insight gleaned from the text and related texts and experiences.

For students who are used to reading assignments that begin with the teacher frontloading most of the information they will need to comprehend a text, such as vocabulary words, elements to look for, or guiding questions, and conclude with teacher-led summaries that point out key ideas and explain what the text means and why it matters, a first encounter with close reading can be a shock. In close reading, it is the students who analyze a text's content and return to it as many times as they need in order to grasp how the language and ideas fit together to support comprehension. However, they must be taught to do so by a very insightful and supportive teacher.

Here are the most important points to remember about close reading:

- Close reading is just one type of classroom reading. Not all the reading students do can or should be close reading, and incorporating close reading into your classroom does not mean that you will no longer provide guided reading instruction with leveled texts, conduct shared readings, lead interactive read-alouds that include modeling and thinking aloud, or divide the class into book clubs for discussion, collaboration, and argument.

- Close reading requires students to become investigators of a short complex text and its meaning and deep structures (Adler & Van Doren (1940/1972). In other words, students work to identify the "bones" of the passage. Because many selected passages may be sections of larger texts, especially when reading a section of a textbook chapter, it is important to be sure that the selected segment contains all the information you are asking students to comprehend. This is often difficult because in a chapter, story, essay, and most text excerpts, meaning is developed while reading the entire text. Also, every reader's interpretation will always be influenced by that reader's prior knowledge and experiences; reading is an interactive process occurring between the reader and the text. For this reason, you must choose selections carefully to maximize every reader's potential to make a connection with the text during the close reading experience.

- Close reading requires students to read and reread, returning to the text at the word, phrase, sentence, and paragraph levels so that they will learn how the text works. The inferences they draw from the text will be supported by their initial and developing knowledge of the topic and by the language and the structure of the text.

- Close reading involves students answering text-dependent questions that keep them focused on what is within the four corners of the text rather than on their personal connections or reactions to the text. While a reader's response to questions asked during close reading should definitely draw from and relate to the information in the text, we must say again that reading is an interaction between the reader and the text, and no one can totally disengage or be encouraged to disengage from prior experiences with a topic, language, and reading process when making inferences during reading about what the text says and means. We believe the authors of the Common Core documents want to move us away from the instructional practice that has become so prevalent in the last few years of asking students to make "text to self" connections—to answer the questions like "How does this text relate to me?" or "What event in my life does this remind me of?" While this practice was never intended to conclude without a return to the text, it too often does. In the classrooms we have visited, we saw many readers spending more time sharing personal experiences than they did talking about the text. During close reading, or any type of reading experience, we must be careful to avoid having readers solely respond to a question using previous experience that is not associated with the text they are reading; emphasis and evidence should be derived from that text. Here, again, we caution you to choose text passages very carefully and, as you write text-dependent questions, to be sure that you consider if students will be able to draw the needed inferences from the selected passage.

Understanding how well each student is able to comprehend the text offers insights to teachers about the instructional scaffolds needed. These scaffolds may be provided through additional text-dependent questions asked during the close reading or in subsequent instruction after close reading. Students will not become proficient readers of complex texts merely by being left to struggle in texts that far exceed their independent reading levels. If we expect them to become proficient, analytical, and independent readers of increasingly complex texts, we must teach them how to apply the knowledge and language they have, how to grow new knowledge and language bases, and how to monitor their understanding of text.

2. How does a close reading experience differ from shared and guided reading instruction?

A close reading experience differs from other reading instruction in several key ways:

- It focuses on short, challenging, complex texts (or challenging and complex sections of larger texts that have self-contained information) within a grade-level Lexile band rather than on grade-level texts.
- It limits the teacher's before-reading activities to a brief text introduction. Teachers do not initially build extensive background or model skills and strategies, as they do during a typical guided, shared, or read-aloud reading lesson.
- It begins with students independently "having a go" at the text—reading it on their own or, if they are beginning readers, listening to the text read

aloud. During this first reading, students may annotate the text (using words, images, or marks) to identify points of confusion, challenging vocabulary, and other noteworthy features. Often, however, students read to get a general understanding of the text information by identifying big ideas and the text's overall structure.

- It features multiple rereadings, guided by text-dependent questions from the teacher, that promote a deepening understanding of how the text works, what it means, and how the information matters or can propel new questions and insights. To answer the questions, students reread the text (or listen to it) multiple times, engaging with it more deeply each time. While questions may be prepared in advance, they are often altered as teachers listen to student responses and conversations, and observe the annotations being made.

- It concludes with written activities, projects, or other experiences designed to extend what students have learned from their examination of the text or to provide opportunities for students to create and share new information from what they have learned. These expressions serve as assessments, providing the teacher with insight into students' subsequent instructional needs.

Figure 2.1 provides a more detailed look at the differences between a typical shared reading lesson and a close reading session, broken out into the familiar "Before, During, and After Reading" structure.

3. What is the purpose of close reading?

When students engage in a close reading, their goal is to gain insight into what the text says, how the message was constructed, and the author's intent. With such insights, a reader can critically and ethically evaluate the text message and how it works. The process of carefully examining the text's language, structure, facts, and details allows students to make the evidence-based inferences about the text's content and structure that are "the heart of meaning construction for learners of all ages" (Anderson & Pearson, 1984, p. 107). By returning to the text multiple times, they have opportunities to deepen this understanding by

- Eliminating ambiguity regarding the text's message
- Analyzing context clues to figure out unfamiliar language
- Noting connections among ideas and key details

Figure 2.1 | **A Comparison of a Shared Reading Lesson and a Close Reading Session**

When	Shared Reading Lesson	Close Reading Session
Before Reading	• The teacher selects a text at or near students' reading levels and sets a purpose for student reading.	• The teacher selects a short, complex "stretch text" at the upper limit of students' grade-level Lexile bands; analyzes it for text complexity; and identifies it to determine possible teaching points that, when addressed through questions and conversations, will support students' analysis of the passage.
	• The teacher builds background knowledge and/or vocabulary before students read.	• The teacher crafts text-dependent questions that will engage students in analyzing the identified points of need and focus—the teaching points.
	• The teacher and students might preview the text together.	• The teacher introduces the context for reading the passage. Teacher limits frontloading of vocabulary and background knowledge.
During Reading	• Depending on grade level, students read or listen to an entire story or passage.	• Depending on grade level, students read or listen to a short text that ranges in length from one paragraph to one page.
	• Students read along and listen to the text being read by the teacher. The teacher determines how to chunk the text and how many times it should be reread. While reading, the teacher might model and think aloud to demonstrate specific reading skills for students before they read. Modeled strategies might illustrate how to make sense of a text; these strategies might include predicting, visualization, questioning, clarifying, and summarizing.	• Students reread the text multiple times for different purposes as related to the text-dependent questions. They annotate as needed.
	• Students practice the modeled skill while reading the text. The teacher or students read a text, stopping to discuss teacher-generated text-independent and text-dependent questions about the text. Students may make text-to-text, text-to-self, and text-to-world connections to the text.	• While reading, students respond to text-dependent questions that focus on what's contained within the text.
		• First Reading: Students "have a go" at the text without teacher background building. Their focus for the reading is based on the lesson purpose and the text-dependent question(s). Teacher may ask students to read without annotating to get the gist or general understanding of the text. They may annotate the text if it naturally supports their analysis.
		• Students share ideas with peers. The teacher listens in and uses student collaborative conversations as formative assessment data to identify areas that are interfering with comprehension; these will become teaching points addressed through subsequent text-dependent questions asked by the teacher.

Continued ➜

Figure 2.1 | **A Comparison of a Shared Reading Lesson and a Close Reading Session (Con't.)**

When	Shared Reading Lesson	Close Reading Session
During Reading	• Students may complete graphic organizers focused on lesson objectives.	• Next Reading: Students reread the text to explore text-dependent questions and deepen their understanding of the passage, vocabulary, text structure, and any other areas the teacher has assessed needs to receive focus. Students annotate the text to address a text-dependent question that focuses them more deeply on how the text language and structure work. The teacher may model a reading skill designed to address the lesson purpose or a teaching point. Students share their annotations and responses with peers. Again, the teacher listens in and assesses their deepening understandings of the textual information. Based on assessments of conversations among the students and their annotations, the teacher asks questions that send them back into the text for a deeper reading. • Additional Readings: Students reread the text again, digging more deeply to answer text-dependent questions related to the meaning of the text, the author's purpose, and/or arguments presented in the text. They may complete graphic organizers or Foldables® during this time.
After Reading	• Students submit a written response to their reading, complete projects, or engage in other activities that demonstrate their comprehension of the text and the modeled strategy.	• Students respond to the text through projects or writing prompts that illustrate their abilities to take a stance, craft an opinion, evaluate a text, develop and support their stance with documented evidence, or create new related information.

- Visualizing the organizational patterns the author used to share information
- Using what they remember to predict what comes next and to stay connected with the passage
- Summarizing aspects of the text as a means to draw conclusions
- Formulating a logical, text-supported evaluation and opinion
- Monitoring their understanding by continually self-assessing if the text is making sense to them and, if it isn't, figure out what is causing the confusion.

Using these insights, readers can be taught how to make a complex text comprehensible, which is exactly what proficient readers do once they no longer have the support of a teacher. It is during these returns to the text that the reader gains deeper insights into the topic and an expanded understanding of the topic and himself or herself as a reader.

In a practical sense, close reading mimics the process readers naturally engage in when attempting to read a text beyond their instructional level without teacher support. First, they look at a text and assess what they know about the topic by activating whatever related knowledge they have about the topic. Then, if they have a purpose for reading the text, they give it a go. If the text is challenging, the reading is seldom if ever "completed" the first time through. Instead, it is read and reread, and during the process, the reader may leave the text and seek to understand language or content through a less difficult, topically related text or source that provides the needed background.

Therefore, as suggested in Chapter 1, close reading is appropriate whenever you determine that the information in a text won't be easily or immediately accessible to your students. They will have to stretch a bit beyond their independent reading level for comprehension to occur. It's also a good choice when your students have some background knowledge that's related to the topic of the text but not enough, in your estimation, to gain a complete understanding of the author's message through just a single reading. It's the experience of returning to the text for analytic study of the message and the author's way of sharing the message that builds the reader's stamina and persistence for wrestling with a challenging text until the meaning and nuances become clear.

4. How often should students engage in close reading?

While there is no definitive answer to this question, we believe that students should engage in daily close reading of texts that represent all areas of the curriculum (language arts, science, social studies, and mathematics). For example, on Monday, students might engage in a close reading in language arts; on Tuesday, they might read closely in social studies, and so on, with close reading incorporated into one of the disciplines each day of the week. Close reading across the disciplines needs to become a habit of practice if students are to develop the skills they need to go beyond a surface reading of texts. Figure 2.2 shows a weekly schedule of close reading designed by a 3rd grade teacher. By making a similar chart and incorporating close reading into the various subjects you teach, you can ensure that your students are learning to closely read many types of texts. See Chapter 4 for more about close reading across the disciplines.

Figure 2.2 | **A Weekly Close Reading Schedule**

Content Area	Monday	Tuesday	Wednesday	Thursday	Friday
Language Arts		Book: Charlotte's Web pp. 10–11			Book: Charlotte's Web p. 42
Science	Book: Where Do Polar Bears Live?				
Social Studies			Book: If the World Were a Village		
Mathematics				Book: Warlord's Puzzle, p. 24	
Other					

5. At what grade level should students be introduced to close reading?

The earlier in their education students begin using the process of close reading or thinking, the more likely it is to become a routine practice they can independently apply whenever they seek to understand a text's deep message and the craft behind it.

We know that many primary teachers become anxious when they hear conversations about close reading. They wonder how they can begin this practice when their students aren't yet able to decode and fluently read even a very short sentence or a text with words that reflect an alphabetically regular consonant-vowel-consonant pattern. When speaking with them, we point out that even kindergarteners and 1st graders can be engaged in close thinking about a challenging text when the teacher reads the text aloud during a shared reading and follows a sequence of instruction that promotes a deeper understanding of the content.

The major difference between close reading in the primary and intermediate elementary grades is that with younger children, the teacher is doing a shared oral reading rather than asking students to read silently, and the students are listening and perhaps following along. While reading the text aloud, the teacher pauses to ask questions that push the students to think deeply about elements of the text as they listen. Then, in repeated rereadings, the teacher might ask a question that draws the students' attention to a particular pattern of language, a key detail that highlights the author's message, a main idea, character traits, how the text relates to another text on the same topic, or any other aspect of the text that is worthy of critical examination.

Teaching early readers to think deeply about a text being read to them will not prevent primary teachers from also teaching the foundational skills of decoding that are critical to reading fluency. By making "close text thinking" an integral component of an early literacy program, right alongside foundational skills, students will acquire the practices of deeply thinking about a text and will be better prepared to do so in their own reading once they *can* fluently decode and process a text.

Another reason to engage students in close reading early in their literacy development is to show them how important it is to use text evidence to support their ideas about that text. The teacher faciliates this by regularly asking questions like *How did you know that? Why do you think that? Why did you say that? Where does it say that? Prove it! Where's the evidence?*

Let's pause to take a look at Figure 2.3, a chart that Lisa Forehand, who teaches a K–1 combination class, used to introduce her young students to the concept and process of close reading.

Ms. Forehand engages her students in closely reading texts early in the year to show them the importance of supporting their ideas with text evidence. The class-created charts (see Figure 2.4) show what the students were thinking about— and the text evidence behind their ideas—as Ms. Forehand read aloud David Shannon's *No, David!* and a book in Eric Litwin and James Dean's *Pete the Cat* series. As the

Figure 2.3 | Close Reading/Thinking Explained for Primary Students

Courtesy of Lisa Forehand.

Figure 2.4 | **Student-Generated Character Analyses**

Courtesy of Lisa Forehand.

children partner talked and shared ideas in response to questions posed prior to each reading, Ms. Forehand charted their responses and documented the character analysis that emerged. Before beginning their close reading of the second book, a little boy named Kona called out excitedly, "We are going to have to think about this character and find EVIDENCE in the book!" To Ms. Forehand, this comment indicated that Kona was very aware of the process of close reading.

Figure 2.5 shows the comparative character analysis Ms. Forehand's K–1 students did of two texts, Kevin Henkes's *Wemberly Worried* and Cynthia Rylant's *The Ticky-Tacky Doll*. Ms. Forehand first read these stories aloud, asking the class to think closely as she read. In a later lesson, she led the students in a comparison for purpose of character analysis. The students in Ms. Forehand's class are well on their way to understanding close reading as a part of their instructional day, and they are familiar with examining text (including illustrations) closely to support their comprehension.

In our conversation with Ms. Forehand, she stated that she believes that closely reading texts with young children is very engaging for them. In her opinion, "Teachers need to look at the texts and resources they already know and have when planning a close reading. As teachers, we all have our 'go-to' pieces for teaching a specific idea or strategy. Take these go-to pieces that we know so well and address the Common Core through them instead of reinventing the wheel and forgetting all we know about teaching students to read. Just be sure that both the selected text and the questions you ask push students to make deeper and deeper inferences. The kids need to go below the surface meaning, and this can sometimes be hard with primary grade texts."

Figure 2.5 | **A Student-Generated Character Comparison**

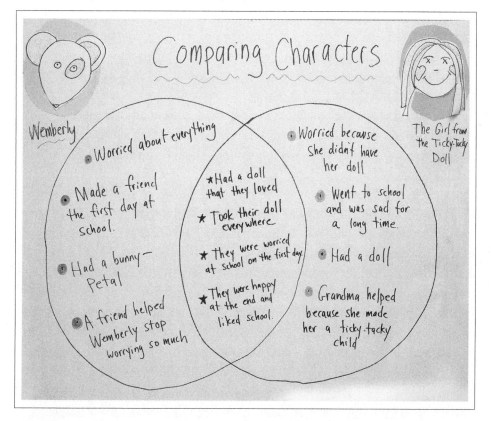

Courtesy of Lisa Forehand.

The Roles of the Reader in the Close Reading Process

An important initial step in teaching students to be close readers is to develop their understanding of close reading as a process and familiarize them with the language associated with thinking closely about a text. This knowledge becomes a foundation for young children on their way to becoming proficient readers of increasingly complex texts—readers who, as Luke and Freebody (1999) note, must engage in four major reading practices, taking on four powerful roles: *code breaker, meaning maker, text user,* and *text critic.*

The reader as code breaker. To be a code breaker, the reader must first understand the alphabetic principle and that the sounds of language are associated with the symbols in a text. Becoming a code breaker involves gaining proficiency with *print concepts, phonological awareness, phonics and word recognition,* and *fluency,* which are identified by the Common Core standards as foundational for learning to read: "These foundational skills are not an end in themselves; rather, they are necessary and important components of an effective, comprehensive reading program designed to develop proficient readers with the capacity to comprehend texts across a range of types and disciplines" (NGA Center & CCSSO, 2010a, p. 15). Being able to apply these code breaking skills means students have the potential to understand a text at a surface or basic level.

The reader as meaning maker. Acquiring automaticity allows the reader to free up working memory to focus on meaning, which is why fluency is an important dimension of comprehension. Samuels (2007) notes that simply teaching students to "bark at words" (or speed read) is not enough to significantly improve their understanding; they must be taught that the print they are reading is bringing them a message from the author. Young readers can begin this process of meaning making as they listen to books read by their teacher and engage in very text-focused conversations that support their deepening understanding of text language, information, and features.

The reader as text user. Thinking beyond the literal or basic level of meaning of the text involves learning to analyze the factors that influenced the author to share the message through the selected text structure. Being a text user means taking control of the reading interaction by returning to the text to think more intensely about the author's message and the language, style, and structures used to convey the message. While doing so, the reader is able to self-assess comprehension and decide which skills to apply in order to accomplish the purpose of reading. Here's an example. Think about your engagement with the text as you read this science passage. Ask yourself: *What is this text saying? What do I already know about this topic? What's new to me? What problems, if any, am I having understanding the author's message?*

> "Eat organic" has become the motto of many families across the nation, but do these consumers really understand what that means? The term *organic*

implies that the farming methods used to produce the foods were focused on creating less pollution and on using less water and soil. In the eyes of most shoppers, this means that chemical fertilizers and insecticides are not used to grow the crops, and that animal antibiotics are not used. Foods may be labeled with a variety of terms, including *100 percent organic* or just *organic*. The first term means 100 percent; the second means at least 95 percent organic. A label stating "Made with organic ingredients" indicates that less than 70 percent of the ingredients are organic.

For some readers, vocabulary may be a roadblock to comprehension. This is particularly true of English language learners. Consider some of the challenging vocabulary in the passage above: *motto, insecticides, antibiotic,* and *indicates.* A text user might go back to reread and focus on these terms, trying to derive meaning through various means, including context and structural analysis. He might even decide that some unfamiliar terms can be mentally noted for future consideration, even if exact definitions cannot yet be determined. When reading *motto,* for example, a reader might not know exactly what the term means, but he could determine that it's something that families think or say, as suggested by the quote marks that surround the motto "Eat organic." Similarly, in analyzing the word *insectides,* the reader might deduce that this term has something to do with insects or bugs. In this passage, the barrier to comprehension could have been language, but other obstacles could also have curtailed reading comprehension.

If the passage had contained many interrelated ideas, developing a graphic organizer might have helped the reader untangle the structure of the message. Or, if the reader determined that the information seemed to be at a more sophisticated level than his current understanding of the topic, he might have sought out and read another, less difficult text on the same topic as a way to gain the knowledge and language needed to return to the more complex passage. Whatever the reader's decisions while reading, being able to make them in support of his own comprehension indicates that he is a metacognitively aware text user who can engage in a conversation with the author by also engaging in a self-directed conversation that considers not only what skills he has that will support his analysis of the author's message but also the skills and knowledge he must develop or acquire.

The reader as text critic. When a reader is able to evaluatively interact with a text, he is functioning as a text critic—someone who understands that the text is not neutral and that the author is attempting to position readers to consider an issue from a specific vantage point. For an example, consider the following headlines. What is each positioning a reader to believe?

- *Is tap water clean enough for you to drink?* This text positions the reader to think that there are cleaner (and, thus, safer or better) alternatives to tap water. The reader must then investigate, perhaps through a review of credible, research-based texts and media resources, whether or not tap water is clean enough to drink.
- *Keeping schools healthy.* This headline, the title of an article in a 1st grade text, positions early readers to think that schools need to do something to keep schools healthy. First grade students may have knowledge about healthy foods and exercise but may not be able to realize that the information they have is what is being referred to in the article title.
- *Global warming is threatening the world's food supply by causing crop pests to move toward the poles.* The headline positions the reader to consider the human impact on our food supply, as global warming is mostly attributed to human use of fossil fuels. The reader must consider the claims that global warming is heating up the Earth and the counterclaims (few that they are) that refute this theory. Additionally, the reader must evaluate whether or not global warming would actually cause crop pests to move toward the poles.

The ability to critically evaluate a text is a sophisticated process that requires practice. Teaching students the process of close reading as a way to scrutinize a text and its relationship with other texts should begin early in a student's school career and should be developed over time and across content areas.

⇛◆⇚

Teaching the process of close reading involves coming to understand it ourselves, and then supporting students through very purposeful instruction that enables them to read closely increasingly complex texts across the disciplines. According to Seymour Papert (quoted in Wurman, 2001), "The role of the teacher is to create the conditions for invention rather than provide ready-made knowledge" (p. 240). Nowhere is this more true than in close reading. In the next chapter, we'll explore the details of planning, conducting, and managing a close reading session.

CHAPTER 3

PLANNING, TEACHING, AND MANAGING CLOSE READING

In this chapter, we move on to the practical work of planning and implementing close reading sessions and the related management and grouping practices. We'll walk through the close reading planning process and then explore two extended examples of close reading in action, one set in a primary classroom and the other in an intermediate elementary classroom. Then we'll delve deeper into classroom management practices and tools to support you as you reflect on your expanding knowledge of close reading practices and implementation.

Please bear in mind that there is no "set in concrete" pattern for planning and conducting a close reading session. The approach we offer is just one of many possibilities, but it is the one we have found to be successful in classrooms throughout the country—appropriate at all grade levels and across the range of student abilities.

Before the Close Reading: Planning and Preparation Practices for Teachers

A close reading session requires careful planning, but it also requires that the teacher be willing to modify the plan based on developing student needs and gains. As explained in Chapter 2's overview of the process and illustrated in the classroom scenarios we will look at in the pages to come, every close reading is shaped not only by the learning goals and the composition of the classroom but also by the students' developing understandings and insights, by the confusions that emerge while encountering a complex text, and by how the teacher accommodates these various factors. To begin, let's look at the planning and preparation work that a teacher should engage in prior to involving students in close reading: (1) determine lesson purpose, tasks, and related standards; (2) select the text; (3) identify the areas of complexity and teaching points; (4) create text-dependent questions; (5) prepare the text for close reading and discussion; (6) model annotation methods; and (7) model how to closely read a text.

Determine the Lesson Purpose, Tasks, and Standards

To begin planning a lesson that involves students in close reading, you will need to first identify the lesson's purpose(s) and tasks, and the related standards. The **lesson purpose** identifies the goal or objective of the lesson, but from a per-spective that clarifies for students the "why" of what they are learning. Sharing the purpose with students helps them to maintain focus on the content. The **lesson tasks** clarify how the purpose is to be accomplished. Careful observation of students' performance in relation to these tasks provides opportunities to assess their growing understandings and skill development. These assessment insights support your next instructional steps. Finally, determining the content and lit-eracy **standards** related to the lesson will provide focus, for both you and your students. You may select a single standard or address several standards within a single lesson.

It's not uncommon to mix up lesson purpose and standards. The key distin-guishing factor is scope. Lesson purpose is smaller-scale and more focused; it's what your students will accomplish during the lesson. By contrast, it's very rare that students will master a standard within a single lesson. For example, a les-son purpose for a close reading might be to *understand various types of rocks.* A related task might be to *write a summary of the reading* or to *share an e-mail with a friend that describes the different rock formations.* This close reading les-son could be one of several lessons designed to accomplish the content standard related to *understanding that the Earth is composed of several layers.*

Select the Text

Selecting a text for a close reading involves careful consideration to ensure that the text not only addresses your identified lesson purpose and standards but is also both engaging and complex enough to push the knowledge levels of students (see Chapter 4). As discussed in Chapters 1 and 4, the complexity level of a text is determined by **quantifiable factors,** such as the number of words in a passage; **qualitative factors,** such as the knowledge demands and language features; and **reader/task factors,** which take into consideration the characteristics of the students who will be reading the text. Texts selected for close reading should be "compact, short, self-contained texts that can be read and reread deliberately and slowly" (Coleman & Pimentel, 2012, p. 4) during a class session. Students might be asked to tackle longer texts at other times in order gain reading stamina and explore their interests.

Other questions to ask when making a selection include the following:

- Does the text or passage contain information that relates to a topic being studied or about to be studied?
- Is the text challenging, interesting, and well-written? As students wrestle with it, will they be seeing a model of writing and language use worth emulating?
- Is the complexity of the text similar to or beyond the students' ability? Will they be stretched by reading it?
- What knowledge will students need in order to read this text? Do they have this knowledge? Does the text offer features, such as context clues, that will support the understanding of readers who don't have much prior knowledge of this topic? If not, how can this information be backfilled?
- Can the entire class closely read this text as it is and on their own, or would some students benefit from reading it partnered with other texts on the same topic to build concepts and language they need for better understanding? Will some students need advance instruction related to the topic in order to build necessary background knowledge, perhaps in a small-group setting? What other supports may be needed?

The goal is that every student will read complex texts at the high end of the grade-level band. However, each student must be supported with very purposeful instructional scaffolds. Most often, these are offered as text-dependent questions that deliberately push students back to sections of the texts to scrutinize author language and related clues that support their deepening understanding.

Determine the Areas of Complexity and Teaching Points

Next, use rubrics similar to those shown in Chapter 1 (see Figures 1.2 and 1.3, pp. 25–30) to identify areas of text complexity that may represent potential problem areas for your students—unfamiliar concepts, layout, vocabulary, language styles, and so on. From there, you must decide if these problem areas require instruction a few days prior to the close reading, or if they will serve as teaching points for the close reading—addressed through the discussions that occur after the first reading, during student conversations, and after subsequent rereadings.

There may be times when it will be clear that your students lack essential information that they will need in order to make sense of the text. For example, if your students are reading a science passage about changes to matter caused by heating and cooling, they will definitely need to understand concepts related to temperature (e.g., *What does hot or cool feel like?*). In these instances, you should preteach this material in a class session prior to your reading session. (It's important not to load students down with information just before their first encounter with the text.)

If you are unsure if students will be able to comprehend these areas of complexity without preteaching, err on the side of letting them try it. In our experience, when students grapple a bit with difficult material, they often generate insights we do not expect. If they stumble during their first reading, help them through collaborative discussion or clarify the information prior to their next reading.

Once you begin the close reading session, you will need to watch and listen carefully to your students, and ask questions that help them grasp the needed information and deepen their understanding of the passage. You can also note which students may need additional supports, which can be provided in a small-group setting. This arrangement is often particularly appropriate for English language learners, who may need the support of both the teacher and their peers to master challenging concepts.

Create Text-Dependent Questions

In close reading, text-dependent questions related to the identified teaching points serve to focus students' interactions with the text. Text-dependent questions differ from the kinds of questions students may be used to answering in response to a reading in that they do not focus on personal connections to the text, but rather require that students focus explicitly on what the text itself has to say. The answers to questions may not be found easily, and answering may require students to read and reread. Questions and prompts that relate to identified teaching points (e.g., *Identify the language that communicates the gist of the author's message*) should be created in a way that returns readers to the text for rereading and deeper analysis (e.g., *What words and phrases tipped you off to what the author really wants us to understand?*). Although it's often recommended that these questions "be answered by careful scrutiny of the text" (Coleman & Pimentel, 2012, p. 5)—that is to say, readers must be true to the meaning suggested in the text—we believe student experience and knowledge also play a role in their ability to connect ideas across texts in order to evaluate the veracity of information in texts. This transaction between the reader and the text (Rosen-blatt, 1978) enables readers to make text-supported judgments as they search, synthesize, infer, and evaluate the texts they are reading in an attempt to analyze an author's message and intention.

Asking students text-dependent questions does not mean asking only low-level, literal questions that involve regurgitation of easy-to-find information. On the con-trary, text-dependent questions should invite students to interpret the theme or major points of information, analyze vocabulary, observe the effects of the author's word choices and use of dialect, and examine the text's structure and features as a means to understand and evaluate the complexity of the message.

After generating a set of questions based on the key ideas, insights, or points they want students to understand from the text (e.g., theme, main idea, persua-sive techniques), the teacher organizes these questions in a way that moves stu-dents from a very literal interpretation of what the text explicitly says to higher levels of analysis, synthesis, and evaluation as they develop insights that enable them to argue a position. Remember, because you will write most of these ques-tions prior to the first reading, you must be prepared to revise them or generate new ones after listening to students' responses.

A simple distinguishing feature of text-dependent questions is that they could not be answered by someone who has not read (or listened to) the particular text. Text-dependent questions differ further from the non–text-dependent ques-tions in that they *push the students back* into the text rather than *take them away* from it. For illustration, consider Figure 3.1, which shows text-dependent and non-text-dependent questions generated for the passage "Owl and the Moon" from Arnold Lobel's *Owl at Home,* a Common Core text exemplar for grades K–1. As you review this figure, also notice that the purpose for each question is indicated. In many instances, these questions will reflect categories found on qualitative scoring rubrics like those we looked at in Chapter 1.

Now let's turn our attention to another example, Figure 3.2's text-dependent and non–text-dependent questions for Leslie Hall's (2009) "Seeing Eye to Eye," a Common Core informational text exemplar identified as appropriate for students in grades 4–5. Again, note how the questions in Column 1 will require readers to return to the passage to find the answers, while those in Column 2 will not.

Also notice that the first of the text-dependent questions really might assess students' general understanding of this text rather than their literal comprehen-sion (their ability to respond "yes" or "no" to a point made in the text), as the non–text-dependent does. Similarly, the second text-dependent question,

Figure 3.1 | **Text-Dependent and Non–Text-Dependent Questions for Lobel's "Owl and the Moon"**

Progression of Questions (Narrative Text)	Text-Dependent Questions	Non–Text-Dependent Questions
General Understanding	What is this story about?	Have you ever seen the moon at night?
Key Details	What did the moon do in the story? How did it move? Where in the story does it tell you this?	What does the moon look like?
Vocabulary	What does it mean when the author writes, "Owl's bedroom was filled with silver light"?	What can you compare the moon to?
Text Structure	Who is talking in this story? How do you know?	If you met the moon, what would you say to it?
Author's Purpose/Message	What is the author trying to tell us by using an owl and the moon as characters?	Why is the moon important to us?
Inferences	How is the presence of the moon like a "good round friend"?	How are your friends like the moon?

Figure 3.2 | **Text-Dependent and Non–Text–Dependent Questions for Hall's "Seeing Eye to Eye"**

Progression of Questions (Informational Text)	Text-Dependent Questions	Non–Text-Dependent Questions
General Understanding	What is the text about?	Are eyes important to vision?
Key Details	Why are eyes important to creatures like falcons and mice?	Do eyes play a role in survival of the fittest?
Vocabulary	How does the author explain the meaning of light?	What science words can you use to describe the parts of a light wave?
Text Structure	What sequencing language does the author use to describe the path of light from an object to the eye?	What comparision words could be used to think about different forms of energy, like light and sound?
Author's Purpose/Message	Why does the author say, "Your eyes are light catchers"?	How is light important to humans and animals?
Inferences	How does the structure of the eye (cornea, lens, retina) help a falcon spot a field mouse that is far away?	Can you see in the dark? Why or why not?
Opinion/Argument	The author writes, "Light rules." How does she explain the rules of light? Provide evidence from the text. Is there sufficient evidence to support the idea that light follows rules?	Does light behave more like a wave or a particle? Explain your ideas.

related to key details, drives students back into the text to see how particular animals, mentioned in the text, benefit from vision. Now look at both questions intended to assess vocabulary. The role of light in vision is addressed in the article, but the non–text-dependent question asks about the anatomy of a wave, a topic related to light but not actually mentioned in this text. The text-dependent vocabulary question on the left asks about a key word that is used. It's the same situation with the text structure questions. The non–text dependent question about text structure is interesting, but it asks for comparison words that are not derived from the text. By contrast, the text-dependent question about text structure asks student to draw from the text to find the language used by the author. Similarly, the inference and argument text-dependent questions require that students look to the text for evidence and clarification, while the non–text-dependent questions can be answered without the text by using other content knowledge. Clearly, the use of well-crafted text-dependent questions is what facilitates the students' closer look at the text and deepens their understanding of text-based content.

Here is one straightforward protocol for generating text-dependent questions:

1. Identify key ideas or concepts in the text.
2. Think about questions that might orient students to the general meanings of the text.
3. Focus on vocabulary and text structure. Determine what key terms and patterns of text structure (problem/solution, compare/contrast, etc.) are used in the text.
4. Determine the most difficult sections of the text, and develop questions that focus on these areas. Consider complex phrasing, dense material, and places where inference is required.
5. Consider the appropriate grade-level versions of Common Core anchor standards and create additional questions to focus students on particular elements of these standards.
6. Develop a series of text-dependent questions that require students to delve deeper with each subsequent reading. Depending on the text, students may need to read or listen to the text multiple times.

Our colleagues Doug Fisher and Nancy Frey (2014) have developed the model shown in Figure 3.3 to guide the creation of text-dependent questions. Their model illustrates a progression that moves from parts to the whole, focusing first on words before expanding to sentences, paragraphs, longer passages, and the text

Figure 3.3 | **A Model for the Progression of Text-Dependent Questions**

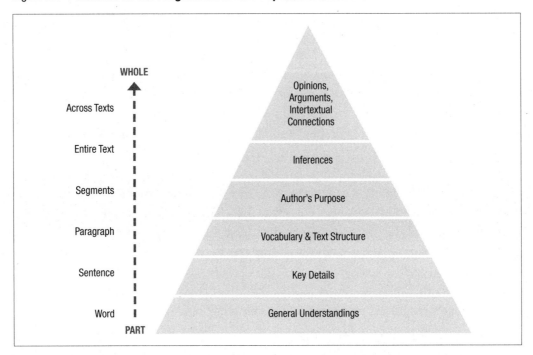

overall. At the same time, they call for these questions to direct students' attention to increasingly sophisticated aspects of the text, moving from key details to the author's purpose to inferences, opinions, and arguments.

While this model identifies a hierarchy of complexity, it is not intended to suggest that teachers must ask a question that addresses each area or that there is only one place to begin. The types of questions that should be asked are dependent on the lesson purpose, the areas of complexity within the text, and the kinds of cognitive and language scaffolding the students need.

We have carried over the categories in Fisher and Frey's model to the template in Figure 3.4, which you might use to jot down a few questions that will support your lesson focus and the skill and knowledge development of your students. Remember, however, that the responses your students generate during the close reading should largely guide the questions you ask. Depending on their initial comprehension and the lesson purpose, you may need to skip some questions or add additional ones. Every plan for close reading evolves because of the performance of the readers.

Figure 3.4 | **A Template for Preparing Text-Dependent Questions**   Download

Progression of Questions (check)	Text-Dependent Questions	Evidence-Based Answers	Page/Para. #
☐ General Understanding ☐ Key Details ☐ Vocabulary and Text Structure ☐ Author's Purpose ☐ Inferences ☐ Opinions, Arguments, Intertextual Connections			
☐ General Understanding ☐ Key Details ☐ Vocabulary and Text Structure ☐ Author's Purpose ☐ Inferences ☐ Opinions, Arguments, Intertextual Connections			
☐ General Understanding ☐ Key Details ☐ Vocabulary and Text Structure ☐ Author's Purpose ☐ Inferences ☐ Opinions, Arguments, Intertextual Connections			
☐ General Understanding ☐ Key Details ☐ Vocabulary and Text Structure ☐ Author's Purpose ☐ Inferences ☐ Opinions, Arguments, Intertextual Connections			

Here's an example of how to use text-dependent questions to direct students' attention to details and concepts and encourage them to evaluate and critique text content. During a close reading of "Seeing Eye to Eye," Angel Washington, a 4th grade teacher, checked in on a conversation between two students working together to answer the following text-dependent question, prepared to help them explore the author's purpose: *Why does the author say, "Your eyes are light catchers"?*

> *Alexandra:* OK: I think she says that because she knows that you have to have light in the room to see.
>
> *Paloma:* Yes, right here it says that "Light from your desk lamp scatters in all directions." So, light has to be in the room. That's why eyes are catchers.

It was clear to Ms. Washington that these students needed additional questions to help them grasp the concept that vision depends on light entering the physical structure of the eye. To focus their thinking in that direction, she followed up with Alexandra and Paloma:

> *Ms. Washington:* It says that light hits the cornea. Where is the cornea? Where in the text does it describe what happens after light hits the cornea? Now think again about why the author says, "Your eyes are light catchers."

Cued to return to the text, Alexandra and Paloma can find the passage explaining that light passes through the cornea, and then *light enters your pupil, the dark center part of your eye.* Ms. Washington hopes that from this, they will derive the idea that light enters the eye—it is "caught" by the eye so it can move through the cornea, to the pupil, through the lens, and then onto the retina.

It's also important to reiterate that although the kinds of questions we are suggesting are answerable with information from the text, as Shanahan (2013) explains, such questions are not always lower-level, *right-there* questions. To the contrary, text-dependent questions can require readers to draw on prior knowledge to intently focus on various aspects of the text. In "Seeing Eye to Eye," a question about the part of the text under the heading "Light Rules" might lead a reader to think of "rules of the road" or the rules of a game—or the guidelines that govern behavior. While drawing on this understanding of rules, the reader might be able to better ascertain which behaviors of light qualify as *rules* (e.g., light travels in straight lines, light moves at 299,700 km/sec) and see how these rules connect to the bigger premise of the article, specifically that *light affects what and how we see.* Additionally, some readers might draw on their understanding of the colloquial expression of approval "That rules!" and consider that perhaps the author is singing the praises of light in addition to discussing its physical rules.

The bottom line is that when you are creating text-dependent questions, regardless of where those questions fall on Bloom's taxonomy, they must compel readers to go back into the text to examine information, data, research, illustrations, charts, and other aspects of the text.

Posting sentence frames on the document camera or the whiteboard or writing them on sentence strips held in a pocket chart are ways to scaffold student responses or focus students on particular aspects of content. Notice how the following sentence frames push responders to use academic vocabulary words and phrases:

> Your eyes are like light catchers because light enters your _____ and then moves through the _____, _____, _____, and then onto the _____.
>
> The author states that your eyes are like light catchers because
> _____.
>
> When the light _____ and then _____, it _____. This is why eyes are considered light catchers.

Frames can be very useful in supporting a range of learners' abilities to talk about a text. You can alter sentence frames to be more or less complex, depending on the needs of the students.

After you have asked questions that continually push the readers back into the text in a way that helps them accomplish the learning targets, most will have a very good understanding of the text. But this doesn't complete the learning process; remember, a primary goal of good instruction is for students to gain the degree of mastery necessary to function on their own, as empowered, independent learners. Therefore, it is important to emphasize that each reader must also become his or her own interrogator during and after a close reading, which means each reader must ask internal questions that are very similar to those that you generate and use to steer students back to the text for deeper understanding. Very young readers will need guidance and support in learning to ask themselves questions of this type, but they are certainly capable of doing so. Here are a few examples of the kinds of questions you want your students to ask themselves:

- What is the author's message at this point in the text?
- What words or phrases are confusing me? Can I find clues from the author to help me understand them?
- What interesting or different ways does the author use language to help me to better understand the message?
- What technique is the author is using to share the information (repetition, questions, italics)?
- Is the message changing throughout the passage?

When the passage being closely read is a story rather than an informational text, readers can ask similar questions that address the features of a narrative (e.g., plot, character development, setting).

With both text types, and regardless of whether you're asking the questions or students are, it's a good idea to require students to provide the evidence that supports their responses. This sheds light on how the reader has come to a specific conclusion and also provides insights for assessment regarding the veracity of the reader's interpretation.

Prepare the Text for Close Reading and Discussion

It's important not to overlook the simple but powerful practice of setting up the texts used for close reading sessions in a way that facilitates directed rereading, discussion, and reference for evidence. This means using a pen, pencil, or sticky notes to number the lines, paragraphs, or stanzas so that it will be easy for everyone to find and refer to the same portion of the text. You can do the numbering in advance for text that will be read aloud or readings that you'll distribute to students, or you can ask the students to number the paragraphs or lines on their own texts before they start reading. When reading text aloud to emerging readers, be sure to use a finger to point to the line or section being read.

Provide Instruction and Modeling on Text Annotation

Text annotation is an essential literacy learning skill and one that is very useful for students during the process of close reading. Annotation promotes active engagement during the act of reading, preventing students from simply skimming a text. When you direct students who are engaging in close reading to look for and annotate aspects of a text that are important to lesson goals, you are facilitating their *attention to* and *understanding of* the text, along with recall of its details, which will support discussion and further exploration.

Of course students (and adults!) can overuse annotation. Many of us have had the experience of returning to a text we annotated by highlighting every other sentence in a different color and wondering *What was I thinking?* There really is no end to what can be annotated: confusing or difficult vocabulary, literary devices (metaphor, simile, imagery, personification, etc.), rhetorical devices and author style (figurative language and dialect, tone, diction, syntax, etc.), text structure (description, sequence, cause/effect, compare/contrast, problem/solution), text features (captions, sequences, footnotes), main ideas, key details, supporting evidence, student questions or areas of confusion, and on and on. Because the possibilities are endless, it's essential to teach students to annotate for distinct purposes and to establish consistency with the markings used within a given class.

Annotations are generally classified into the following categories: language, questions, predictions, opinions, author's craft, author's message, connections, reflections, and arguments. For example, when reading to focus on language, students might circle confusing words (marking them with a *C*) and interesting words (marking them with an *I*).

Individual close reading sessions frequently include some guidance and modeling of text annotation, even if it's just to remind students of the classroom's standard markings and symbols. But because many students in grades K–5 may be new to the practice, it's worth taking a look at how to teach students to annotate well. Figure 3.5 shows two charts that were posted in classrooms to introduce students to consistent text annotation and provide an ongoing reference. Note how both show the symbols for each category of annotations being used. The arrow on the primary classroom chart identifies the particular annotation feature the teacher and students were practicing when the photo was taken.

When introducing text annotation to students, model for them the features to consider while reading. For example, explain that annotations help us return to a text to clarify confusing words, questions we have, important features and points within the text, language we like, and so on. Also explain that it's important to use a consistent pattern of markings so it's easier to remember which features we were thinking about while reading. Provide students with time to practice and discuss the annotations and how they help support conversations about text, rereadings of text, and writing about text.

Figure 3.5 | **Annotation Chart Examples**

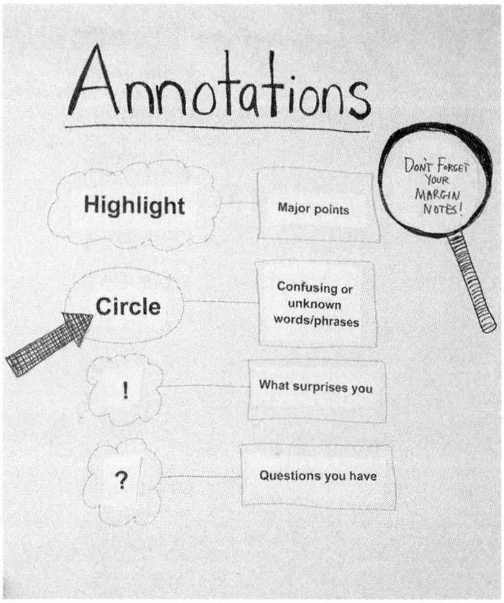

| In a Primary Classroom | In an Intermediate Classroom |

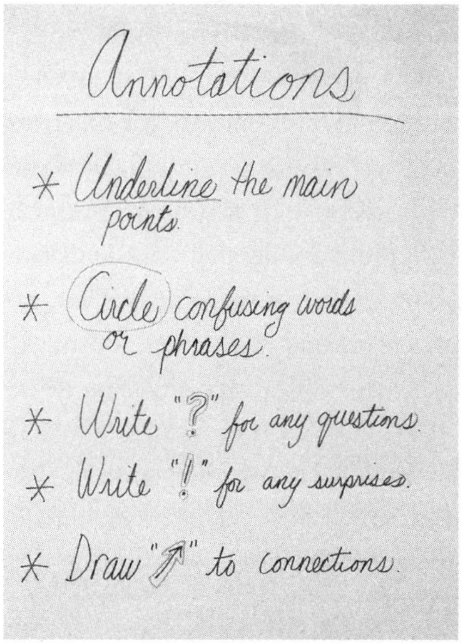

Once you have finished modeling how to annotate a text and students have practiced various text annotations, invite them to give it a try. Using a new passage, have them read and annotate. Remind them to refer to the annotation chart as needed. Have them discuss their annotations with a peer, and then spend a few minutes doing this as a class to be sure that everyone understands and is using the same system and symbols. As students grow more comfortable with reading and annotating, you might experiment with allowing multiple annotations at the same time. For example, during the same reading, you might have students circle unfamiliar words and also include questions next to ideas that are unclear. When students have become comfortable with the annotation system you use in your classroom, you may want to encourage them to add new symbols of their own, as needed.

Another mode of annotation, referred to earlier, is highlighting different features in a text with different colors. For example, students might highlight unfamiliar words in yellow, and language that identifies the author's position on a topic in green. This method of color-coding must be consistent, of course, and it must appear on the annotation chart. Colored pencils can also be used to circle and underline key words or phrases that relate to the identified purpose. They're often a better choice than highlighters, because a student reading with a colored pencil in hand is much more likely to add related margin notes than a student reading with a highlighter. While it's fine for younger students to simply circle a phrase and put a *?* in the margin, intermediate students are old enough to capture their thoughts on the page, whether these are questions, predictions of confusing words, or connections made to other parts of the text. As the students work to make sense of complex text, these notes may be more helpful than relying just on symbols and letters. Of course, students who are English language learners, striving readers and writers, or very young can benefit enormously from making even simple annotations or by using sketches to annotate.

If you are having students closely read and annotate passages within their textbooks, you may want to pass out photocopies of the pages in question for students to mark up and store in their textbooks. This gives them a durable record of their reading thoughts in a form that preserves the surrounding supports of the textbook's pictures, charts, and graphs, which is especially beneficial when reading science or social studies texts, as the visuals help to support students' analysis.

Model How to Closely Read a Text

Teaching students to closely read a text begins by modeling the close reading practices in which students should engage, and ends with students being able to independently apply these practices whenever they read closely. Because close reading skills are developed over time, modeling the process is not a "one and done" situation; you should expect to model close reading both when you first introduce the practice to students and as needed prior to and during subsequent close reading sessions.

Here's a look at how Lin Ryan modeled close reading to introduce the process to her 3rd graders. For her first modeling, Ms. Ryan selected a passage on a topic that she found interesting:

Flooding Causes Engineers to Think of Solutions

1. Recent flooding of the Missouri River has created problems for farmers
2. and homeowners all over Fremont County. Iowa corn farmer Jed Marshall
3. noted, "We have a big problem when it rains for days. If the land gets
4. saturated, then water just sits on top, causing the corn to be destroyed." To
5. battle this problem, engineers are focusing on repairing damaged levees and
6. building new ones.

The teacher began by explaining to her students that the topic of river flooding was one that she had been hearing lots about, both in the popular press and from her friends. She realized that she didn't know enough about the topic to be able to engage in conversation about it. Ms. Ryan explained that she had decided to teach herself more about the causes and impact of river flooding, and that in order to do that, she needs to read articles about the topic very closely to be sure that she is understanding them. "I'm going to show you how I conduct a close reading," she told the class.

As Ms. Ryan read the passage, she annotated and thought aloud about the text by analyzing the language and message. In particular, she noted that the term *saturated,* in line 4, was new to her. She noticed the use of the problem/solution text structure (through the use of if/then), and commented on the fact that engineering was connected to science. Speaking aloud, she asked herself questions that caused her to reread a line or two: "Why is too much water bad for corn? I'm going to reread to find this out." She concluded by discussing with students how the close analysis of the text language and organization helped her gain initial insights about the author's message, and how she gained an even deeper understanding by returning to the passage for additional rereadings. Specifically, Ms. Ryan noted that while some water is good for crops, too much can destroy them. She added that she thinks that the engineers were the ones to find solutions to the problems of the farmers by building a new levee and identifying a way to repair damaged ones.

Once Ms. Ryan's students seemed comfortable with the practice of close text reading, she felt confident in releasing the responsibility for subsequent close text readings to them. However, she knew that modeling would continue to be a valuable tool her whenever her students struggled to apply a new strategy or grasp new content.

During the Close Reading: An Illustration of Teacher and Student Practices

Figure 3.6 provides an overview of teacher and student practices throughout the whole close reading process: before, during, and after the session. Notice that the first five practices of the teacher—the planning work of identifying the

Figure 3.6 | **Close Reading Practices of Teachers and Students**

When	Teacher Practices	Student Practices
Before the Session *(Pre-planning and preparation work)*	1. Select an appropriate text that relates to the identified lesson pupose. 2. Identify potential problem areas and teaching points. 3. Create text-dependent questions. 4. Prepare the text for close reading. 5. Model annotation methods and close reading, as necessary.	
During the Session	6. Ask text-dependent questions. 7. Promote rich and rigorous conversations that support the lesson purpose(s). 8. Observe student's oral and written responses to identify the next appropriate question to ask. 9. Invite rereadings as needed to support students' deep text analysis. 10. During each reading, collect observational data to determine the next questions and instructional paths to support students' analysis. 11. Backfill rather than frontload information through questions that draw students' attention to the text meaning and workings (i.e., language structure, purpose, and intent). 12. Ensure that conversations and experiences connect to the text and the lesson purposes. 13. Initiate a "best use" activity that invites students to share their understandings and create new information.	1. Read, analyze, and annotate the text for a specific purpose. 2. Engage in focused, collaborative conversations that address an identified purpose. 3. Reread to expand understanding about the text. 4. Converse with others to share interpretations and seek clarity. 5. Reread and continue collaborations as needed until a deep understanding of the text features and author's message is achieved.
Beyond the Session	14. Encourage students to employ close reading practices independently. 15. Meet with small groups as needed to ensure that everyone has deeply comprehended the text.	6. Complete a "best use" activity to illustrate a deep understanding and use of the text information. 7. Understand the value of the practice of close reading well enough to apply it without the involvement of others.

lesson purpose and standards, selecting a text, determining potential problem areas, generating text-dependent questions, and any preparatory text annotation or close reading modeling required—should occur *before* students see the passage to be closely read. Teacher practices 6–15 support students *during* and *after* the close reading. We'll now explore both through classroom scenarios. As you read these, be sure to pay attention to how the questions the teachers ask correspond to the identified teaching points.

A Look at Close Reading and Thinking in 1st Grade

Before the reading. Jan Greenfield's 1st graders are just learning to negotiate complex texts. To help them move forward in their reading, she conducted a close reading of an informational text that explains the movement of the sun and moon across the sky (see Figure 3.7).

To ensure that she properly identified potential problem areas for readers, Mrs. Greenfield used the Qualitative Scoring Rubric for Informational Text (see Figure 1.3, p. 28) to analyze the text. Her assessment of the text yielded this information:

- *Text Structure—Organization:* Challenging/stretch text; organization includes multiple text structures, including those that indicate a chronology or conditions or time sequence (*in the morning, by evening*), cause/effect, problem/solution, description, directions, compare/contrast.
- *Text Structure—Visual Supports and Layout:* Moderate/at grade level; text is partnered with illustrations of the sun and moon in the sky at different times of day.
- *Text Structure—Relationships Among Ideas:* Moderate/at grade level; relationships are sometimes implied—for example, the author states that the moon moves across the sky like the sun. Students might infer that the moon rises and sets. Also, they might infer that the sun is seen during the day and the moon is seen at night.
- *Language Features—Author's Style:* Challenging/stretch text; the style is specialized to science (several complex sentences such as *By evening, when it's time to eat dinner and go to bed, it has moved.*)
- *Language Features—Vocabulary:* Moderate/at grade level; discipline specific with some unfamiliar science words and academic language—words like *higher up, disappears,* and *hanging.*
- *Meaning:* Moderate/at grade level; some information is complex (patterns of movement of sun and moon over the course of a day)

Figure 3.7 | **A Primary Text Prepared for Close Reading**

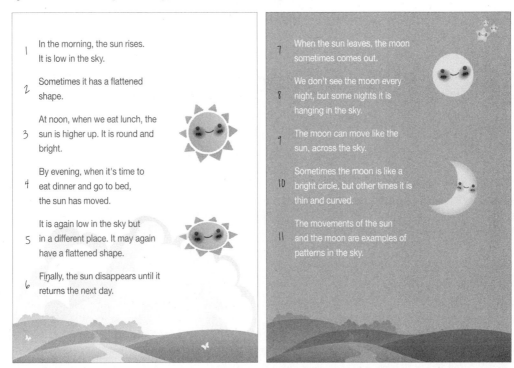

1 In the morning, the sun rises. It is low in the sky.

2 Sometimes it has a flattened shape.

3 At noon, when we eat lunch, the sun is higher up. It is round and bright.

4 By evening, when it's time to eat dinner and go to bed, the sun has moved.

5 It is again low in the sky but in a different place. It may again have a flattened shape.

6 Finally, the sun disappears until it returns the next day.

7 When the sun leaves, the moon sometimes comes out.

8 We don't see the moon every night, but some nights it is hanging in the sky.

9 The moon can move like the sun, across the sky.

10 Sometimes the moon is like a bright circle, but other times it is thin and curved.

11 The movements of the sun and the moon are examples of patterns in the sky.

- *Author's Purpose:* Moderate/at grade level; the purpose is subtle and requires interpretation; students may be able to determine that this is about patterns in the sky.
- *Knowledge Demands:* Moderate/at grade level; students have some background knowledge because most know the sun moves in the sky. They have talked about this in class.

Given this analysis, Mrs. Greenfield concluded that the text was overall at a moderate level of complexity, with some elements that would require students to stretch their thinking. She prepared by crafting text-dependent questions that addressed the potential areas of need. For example, she planned to have students go back into the text with her for second and third readings so that they could respond to the following questions: (1) *Where does the author use words that tell you where the sun is in the sky at different times of day?* (e.g., in the morning, at noon, when we eat lunch); (2) *The author talks about how the moon moves. What sentence tells you about this?*

First reading and discussion. Because 1st graders generally do not have the fluency or automaticity to engage in an independent close reading of a text, Mrs. Greenfield's task during the first close reading was to engage them in closely thinking about the text as they listened to it read aloud.

Mrs. Greenfield began her close, shared reading by explaining to students that they would be learning about how the sun and moon move across the sky. She displayed the pages on the document camera so all could see the text and illustrations. She prompted the children to closely listen for information that identified the following questions: *Where is the sun in the sky in the morning? Where is the sun in the sky at noon? Where is the sun in the sky in the evening?* To support their efforts to answer these questions, she distributed copies of the Foldable® shown in Figure 3.8, and invited students to draw and write their responses on this graphic organizer.

During first readings, Mrs. Greenfield typically just asks the children to listen to get the general gist of what is happening in the text. With this text, however, she felt they were ready for an initial deeper analysis because they had already spent time in class talking about the sky, stars, and moon. Opening the book, Mrs. Greenfield read aloud chunks of the text, moving slowly through the lines (numbered in advance) and showing the accompanying illustrations. Stopping every few sentences, she asked children to annotate by writing or drawing on their Foldable what they remembered about the text they had just heard. After students analyzed content independently, they partner-shared their Foldables with one another, pointing out the details they remembered.

Figure 3.8 | **A Primary Grade Foldable© Graphic Organizer**

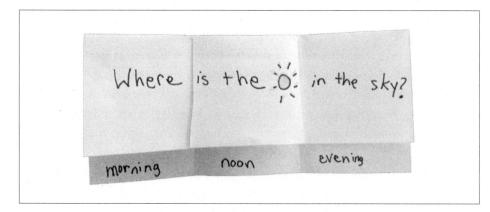

Next reading and discussion. The students listened as Mrs. Greenfield reread the sentences focused on how the moon looks and moves across the sky (lines 9–11). She asked the students to review their drawings and add details or words they had learned from the text. Some students labeled pictures with the words they saw in the text—*morning, noon, evening.*

Mrs. Greenfield then invited partner talk, during which students shared their labeled pictures and ideas. As they did so, Mrs. Greenfield listened in to provide support, assess developing understanding, and determine her next instructional steps. Because she noticed that some students struggled with sequencing information (she had predicted as much in her preparation for this close reading), she asked this text-dependent question: *Where does the author use words that tell you where the sun is in the sky at different times of day?* As students responded, Mrs. Greenfield helped to clarify the times of day by having individuals point out key words projected on the whiteboard. She then shared pictures to correlate these terms with times of day. For example, when Jessica pointed to *morning,* Mrs. Greenfield shared a picture of a child waking up and yawning in the morning. For *noon,* she shared a photo of children eating lunch in the cafeteria. Her *evening* photo depicted a family eating dinner. Mrs. Greenfield made a note that many students were not familiar with the term *evening.* She also noted that the pictorial representations of words were particularly supportive for the many English language learners in the classroom.

Subsequent reading and discussion. Once students understood the content, Mrs. Greenfield wanted them to focus on the craft the author used to share the text information. Specifically, she wanted students to notice the author's use of descriptive language—words like *flattened, round, bright,* and *curved.* Addressing Reading Standard RI.1.4 ("Ask and answer questions to help determine or clarify the meaning of words and phrases in a text"), she gave this prompt: *What words does the author use to describe how the sun and moon look?* She read through the text aloud again, pausing as she did so to ask more questions about the author's choice of words: *What words does the author use to help you know what the sun looks like in the morning, at noon, and in the evening? What shapes does the moon have on different nights?*

After students had heard and thought about the text multiple times, as prompted, Mrs. Greenfield introduced an additional and challenging text-dependent question intended to help them think more deeply about the text: *How does the movement of the sun and the moon show patterns?* By asking this question, she was also addressing Reading Standard RI.1.3 ("Describe the connection between two individuals, events, ideas, or pieces of information in a text"). For students, the challenge was to use their knowledge of patterns, a topic they had discussed previously, to connect daily movements of celestial bodies in the sky to the notion of patterns. Mrs. Greenfield invited individuals to come to the whiteboard and point to the sections of the text that had informed their explanation. They discussed clues in the text, such as the last sentence, which connected "movements we see every day" to the idea of patterns.

Writing activity. Satisfied that her students all understood the information in the text, Mrs. Greenfield asked them to complete the following language frame, referring to the information they'd found in the text and captured in their Foldables:

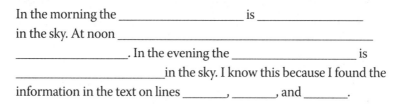

In the morning the _____ is _____
in the sky. At noon _____
_____. In the evening the _____ is
_____in the sky. I know this because I found the
information in the text on lines _____, _____, and _____.

Once students finished their writing, they shared it with others at their table. In this lesson, Mrs. Greenfield provided her 1st graders with opportunities to use academic language during their close reading and thinking, their peer collaborations, and their writing. She did this while addressing multiple standards.

A Look at Close Reading in 5th Grade

Before the reading. Jim Moore set out to build his 5th grade students' ability to analyze an author's style and use of language. He knew he wanted to give them the opportunity to struggle a bit with how word choice and usage help a reader visualize a story's setting and characters. He also wanted to share a wonderful example of a complex literary text that would inspire students' own descriptive writing. To address these lesson purposes, he chose an excerpt from Grace Lin's *Where the Mountain Meets the Moon* (2009), shown in Figure 3.9.

Figure 3.9 | **An Intermediate Text Extract Prepared for Close Reading**

1   Far away from here, following the Jade River, there was once a
black mountain that cut into the sky like a jagged piece of rough
metal. The villagers called it Fruitless Mountain because nothing
grew on it and birds and animals did not rest there.

2   Crowded in the corner of where Fruitless Mountain and the Jade
River met was a village that was a shade of faded brown. This
was because the land around the village was hard and poor. To
coax rice out of the stubborn land, the field had to be flooded
with water. The villagers had to tramp in the mud, bending and
stooping and p   g day after day. Working in the mud so much
made it spread everywhere and the hot sun dried it onto their
clothes and hair and homes. Over time, everything in the village
had become the dull color of dried mud.

3   One of the houses in this village was so small that its wood
boards, held together by the roof, made one think of a bunch
of matches tied with a piece of twine. Inside, there was barely
enough room for three people to sit around the table—which was
lucky because only three people lived there. One of them was a
young girl called Minli.

4   Minli was not brown and dull like the rest of the village. She had
glossy black hair with pink cheeks, shining eyes always eager
for adventure, and a fast smile that flashed from her face. When
people saw her lively and impulsive spirit, they thought her
name, which meant quick thinking, suited her well. "Too well,"
her mother sighed, as Minli had a habit of quick acting as well.

Source: From *Where the Mountain Meets the Moon* (pp. 1–2) by Grace Lin, 2009, New York: Little, Brown Young Readers.
Copyright © 2009 by Little, Brown. Reprinted with permission.

Like Mrs. Greenfield, Mr. Moore identified potential problem areas prior to the close reading session. Using the Qualitative Scoring Rubric for Narrative Text (see Figure 1.2, p. 25), he planned his lesson based on the following general assessment of the text and his students:

- *Text Structure—Organization:* Moderate/at grade level; organization includes narrative text structures that describe, such as "the land around the village was hard and poor."
- *Text Structure—Visual Supports and Layout:* Moderate/at grade level; text includes full-color drawings at the beginning of each chapter.
- *Text Structure—Relationships Among Ideas:* Moderate/at grade level; relationships are sometimes implied in this text. For instance, the author writes that "her mother sighed, as Minli had a habit of quick acting as well," implying that Minli's mother believes she acts before she thinks.
- *Language Features—Author's Style:* Challenging/stretch text; several complex sentences might interfere with students' understanding because of the use of commas and dashes. The last sentence may confuse students if they do not know to what "Too well" refers.
- *Language Features—Vocabulary:* Challenging/stretch text; many words, such as *coax, twine,* and *impulsive,* might challenge students.
- *Meaning:* Moderate/at grade level; some information is complex (villagers coax rice out of the stubborn land; they are bending and stooping day after day).
- *Author's Purpose:* Challenging/stretch text; the purpose requires some interpretation; students may not be able to determine that this passage shows contrasts between the setting and the character.
- *Knowledge Demands:* Moderate/at grade level; students have some background knowledge about folktales, dragons, magic, and adventures.

Given this analysis, Mr. Moore chose to focus his lesson on how the author used language to help the reader visualize the setting and the characters. As shown in Figure 3.10, he prepared a set of text-dependent questions and evidence-based answers to help students achieve the lesson purpose of visualizing the setting and characters. He knew that these questions and answers were just a place to start; he might need to add or skip questions based on his students' understanding. Notice how these questions steer the reader to a deeper understanding of the text's language.

Figure 3.10 | **Text-Dependent Questions and Evidence-Based Answers for Lin's *Where the Mountain Meets the Moon***

Progression of Questions (check)	Text-Dependent Questions	Evidence-Based Answers	Page/Para. #
☑ General Understanding ☐ Key Details ☐ Vocabulary and Text Structure ☐ Author's Purpose ☐ Inferences ☐ Opinions, Arguments, Intertextual Connections	What is happening in this passage?	A girl lives in a poor village near a mountain. The people in the village work hard.	Paragraphs 1–4
☐ General Understanding ☑ Key Details ☐ Vocabulary and Text Structure ☐ Author's Purpose ☐ Inferences ☐ Opinions, Arguments, Intertextual Connections	What is the setting of this passage? Who is mentioned in the passage?	Fruitless Mountain, Jade River, village The villagers, Minli, and her mother.	Paragraph 1 Paragraphs 2–4
☐ General Understanding ☐ Key Details ☐ Vocabulary and Text Structure ☑ Author's Purpose ☐ Inferences ☐ Opinions, Arguments, Intertextual Connections	What words does the author use to describe the characters? What is the purpose for using these words to describe Minli?	Villagers – brown and dull Minli –glossy black hair, pink cheeks, shining eyes These words describe someone who is full of life, and ready for adventures.	Paragraph 4 Paragraph 4
☐ General Understanding ☐ Key Details ☑ Vocabulary and Text Structure ☑ Author's Purpose ☐ Inferences ☐ Opinions, Arguments, Intertextual Connections	Why would the author choose to name the river Jade and the mountain Fruitless?	Jade is the color of green and this is in contrast to the black Fruitless Mountain. These two settings contrast with one another just as Minli con-trasts with the other villagers.	Paragraphs 1–4

Mr. Moore also prepared for sharing the lesson by copying the short passage on legal-size paper so students would have space to add margin notes in addition to highlighting, underlining, and circling words and phrases. On their copies of the passage, students could annotate major ideas, confusing words, surprises, and questions to deepen their understanding of the setting and the characters.

First reading and discussion. Mr. Moore began the lesson by stating the purpose: "As we read today, I want you to pay close attention to how the author's language helps us visualize the setting and characters. Let's number our paragraphs and then do a first reading to just get a feeling for what is happening in the text."

Mr. Moore's students were used to reading a text closely. Some chose to annotate (highlight, circle, and underline words) during the first reading, while others read without annotating. When they finished, Mr. Moore checked for general understanding of the passage by asking what was happening in the text. Students talked in pairs and at their tables about what they had read. Mr. Moore moved among the small groups, listening in to decide which of the text-dependent questions he had prepared would move the group to a deeper understanding. As he walked around and listened in, he used an observation form like the one in Figure 3.11 to capture data on the students' annotations and conversations that would inform his next set of questions and next instructional moves. We will take a closer look at the process of formative assessment during close reading in Chapter 6.

Next reading and discussion. Because Mr. Moore's students were not precisely identifying the language that was key in understanding the difference between the setting and the character, he asked them to return to the text a second time to pay close attention to any words, phrases, or details that helped them create vivid mental pictures of the setting and character: "What words describe the mountain and the village so well that you can picture these? What words make you see the character Minli?"

Mr. Moore specifically wanted students to notice the key language details the author used when describing the setting and the character. He asked students to annotate by circling words that described the setting and underline words that described the character. After they had read and annotated the passage a second time, he invited them to work with a partner to complete the graphic organizer shown in Figure 3.12.

Figure 3.11 | **An Observation Form for Formative Assessment of Close Reading**

Download

Text: _____

Date: _____

Preplanned Text-Dependent Questions	Observations of Students *Who is confused?* *What are the misconceptions?*	New Text-Dependent Questions to Further Student Understanding

Figure 3.12 | **A Graphic Organizer for Capturing Text Evidence**

Vivid Language That Helps Me See What I Read	
Text evidence describing the setting	Text evidence describing the character

Students in this 5th grade class were accustomed to transferring annotations and margin notes to a graphic organizer. As they charted and chatted, Mr. Moore had another opportunity to gather formative assessment data on his students' progress toward accomplishing the lesson purpose. Observing that they were now attending to the precision of the author's language choices, Mr. Moore said, "Now that you have added some words that help you to visualize the setting and characters, please add to your graphic organizer, recording a *P* next to the words and phrases that created positive visual images in your mind and an *N* next to those that are negative."

Students were able to identify and label some of the more obviously positive and negative words and phrases, such as *shining eyes, adventure, hard and poor,* and *the dull color of dried mud*. Mr. Moore knew at this time that another read was necessary in order for the students to understand the author's juxtaposition of the setting and character. An example of this is found in Paragraph 2: *Villagers had to tramp in the mud . . . bending and stooping . . . hot sun dried* [mud] *onto the* [villagers'] *clothes and hair and homes.* These negative images are in contrast to some of the phrases in Paragraph 4 that state that Minli is *lively and quick thinking*.

Additional readings and discussion. Students had read this text twice on their own, and Mr. Moore felt that *his* fluent reading might help them uncover some of the less obvious positive and negative visual images that could help them understand the juxtaposition of the setting and the character. Rather than read the whole text, he read the first two paragraphs, pausing to show students which words he was adding to his graphic organizer and why. Mr. Moore pointed out how *Jade River* could be added to his graphic organizer as a phrase that generates positive images, while *jagged piece of rough metal, bending and stooping,* and *dried mud in hair* could be added to the graphic organizer as phrases creating negative images.

Because his students were nodding and had expressions of understanding on their faces, Mr. Moore decided they were ready to tackle the remaining paragraphs on their own. Students continued to add to their graphic organizer words and phrases such as *shining eyes* and *fast smile* that were not as obvious during the first two readings.

Mr. Moore believed students were ready to be pushed back into the text to consider the author's use of foreshadowing. His next instructional purpose was to prompt his students with questions about how the author used language to help foreshadow future events in the text. "Think about how the author describes Minli," he said. "Were you surprised by the last line of the text? Why or why not? How does it fit with or contradict what the author wrote about Minli in the previous paragraphs? What would be the purpose of using contrasting language when describing the main character and describing where the main character resides?"

Writing activity. As an exit slip for this lesson that would also be used for formative assessment, Mr. Moore asked students to respond to the following prompt: *What language does the author use to describe Minli, and how might this language help foreshadow what will we read about tomorrow?* Students were encouraged to complete their written response using the following sentence frames, if needed:

The author uses _____ to help me understand that _____.

Minli is described as _____. This creates a _____ visual image.

By using the words _____ and phrases _____, the author is foreshadowing that _____.

Both of the classroom examples offered here are intended to provide insight into the process of close reading and one way it might be planned and implemented. We encourage you to create a close reading structure that works for your students and is adaptable enough to address the teaching points of the text you are using. For example, your students may need to read some passages twice and other texts more than twice. The focus and details of a close reading always depend on the text, the lesson purpose, and the reader's familiarity with the topic of the passage. Some texts might contain language that requires in-depth attention, while others might require more attention to key details. Ultimately, the reason for rereading is to help students to not only understand the key ideas and details of the message but also develop awareness of how the message was conveyed by the author.

The **Planning Guide for Close Reading**, shared in Figure 3.13, can serve as a resource for planning and conducting your next close reading.

Managing Close Reading

Now that we've examined the process of close reading in action, let's address just how close reading fits into a daily classroom schedule and how to employ it in a way that will accommodate different student strengths and grouping arrangements.

Scheduling: Making Close Reading an Integral Part of the School Day

If teachers are going to engage students in close reading on a daily basis, they need to make this practice a regular part of the weekly schedule alongside other reading instruction like read-alouds, shared reading, guided reading, and independent reading experiences.

One way to make close reading part of your schedule is to regularly substitute close reading experiences for one of these commonly used literacy learning experiences. For example, in grades K–5, shared readings are very common. Some teachers do these daily. Try substituting one close reading lesson that extends over several days for one or more shared readings. In the same way, you might conduct a close reading once or twice a week during the time usually used for guided reading groups. In this set up, students can begin the close reading experience in a large-group setting and follow-up with small-group guided reading experiences for the second or third readings.

Figure 3.13 | **A Planning Guide for Close Reading**

Download

CLOSE READING PRE-PLANNING

Lesson Purpose:_____

Common Core State Standard(s):_____

Date:_____ Grade:_____ Discipline: _____

Step 1: Select the Text

Text should be short, complex, and worthy of a close read. Remember to include a wide range of genres over time.

Title:

Author:

Page(s) or chunk(s) of text:

Step 2: Determine the Areas of Complexity/Potential Problem Areas and Teaching Points

Think about your students and aspects of the text that may interfere with their comprehension. Those chosen should become the focus of your teaching points. Refer to your qualitative rubric.

Literary Texts	Informational Texts
○ Text Structure	○ Text Structure
○ Language Features	○ Language Features
○ Meaning	○ Meaning
○ Author's Purpose	○ Author's Purpose
○ Knowledge Demands	○ Knowledge Demands

Step 3: Generate Text-Dependent Questions

Develop several high cognitive level questions that you may ask, depending on students' conversations with you and each other. Questions should require students to use the author's words. Prompt students to use text evidence. Use the progression of text-dependent questions as a scaffold. Focus on those that will best support your students in acquiring the knowledge needed to expand their comprehension.

1. _____

2. _____

3. _____

4. _____

5. _____

6. _____

Continued ➜

Figure 3.13 | **A Planning Guide for Close Reading (Con't.)**

Download

CLOSE READING SESSION

Remember to number the paragraphs or chunks of text. Limit frontloading when introducing the text.

First Reading

The first reading of a text should allow the reader to gain a general understanding of what the text says. If your students are in grades K–2, you may need to read the text while they listen and think closely. Encourage students to annotate while reading to identify big ideas, if that is your initial focus. You may also want to use the first reading to have students identify (circle) words that are difficult for them. This provides insight into comprehension interference. Base your direction during the first reading on your prior assessment of the text complexity as it relates to your students.

Purpose Setting: Let's read to find out . . .

○ Teacher Read   ○ Student Read

First Discussion: Partner talk and check meaning

Students dialogue about their understanding of the text or about the difficult text language, if that was your direction to them. Listen, and assess what students have understood. The next questions asked should build from these insights.

Next Reading

Based on the responses of the students, ask a question or two that pushes them back to the text to expand their thinking. This reading of the text should focus the reader's attention on how the text works by prompting consideration of author's use of language and the structure of the text. Encourage students to annotate while attending to text-dependent questions.

Text-Dependent Question:
Evidence-Based Answer (include p. # or para. #):

Text-Dependent Question:
Evidence-Based Answer (include p. # or para. #):

Next Discussion: Partner talk and check meaning
Students dialogue about their understanding and language of the text at a deeper level. Listen and assesses what students have understood and determine what next questions to ask.

Additional Readings

Additional readings of the text should allow the reader to draw inferences and make intertextual connections through a deepening understanding of the text's language, structure, and meaning. Encourage students to annotate while attending to text dependent questions.

Text-Dependent Question:
Evidence-Based Answer (include p. # or para. #):

Text-Dependent Question:
Evidence-Based Answer (include p. # or para. #):

Additional Discussions: Partner talk and check meaning
Students dialogue about their understanding of the text at this deepened level. Listen and assess what students have understood and determine whether more text-dependent questions and additional readings are needed.

Writing as an Assessment and/or to Extend Meaning

A writing activity allows students to demonstrate their understanding of the text and serves as a performance assessment.

For example, Marla Chou wanted her 2nd graders to do a close reading of Chapter 1 of the text exemplar *Cowgirl Kate and Cocoa* by Erica Silverman. While this book has a Lexile measure of 400L, slightly below the range for a complex text in grade 2, Ms. Chou used the Qualitative Scoring Rubric for Narrative Text/Literature (see Figure 1.2, p. 25) to identify a number of potential areas of challenge that would be teaching points in her lesson. For example, she noted four potential areas of difficulty for her students:

1. The use of compound words (*cowgirl, cowhorse, saddlebag*) critical to understanding the story
2. The use of multiple-meaning words, like range and coat
3. The amount of dialogue and how the speakers switched back and forth
4. The story's ranch setting, which would be unfamiliar to many of her students

Ms. Chou's lesson purpose was for students to "use information gained from the illustrations and words in a text to demonstrate understanding of the . . . setting" (RL.2.7).

This close reading experience spanned several days, which is often the case for students in the primary grades who need to spend time working on foundational decoding and interpreting skills as part of the close reading. For the first close reading of the chapter, Ms Chou directed students to annotate the text to identify key terms and ideas they did not understand.

Many students were confused about key vocabulary related to the setting, like *ranch, range, mane, cowgirl, herd,* and the dialogue between Kate and Cocoa. On the second day of instruction, following the large-group first reading and annotation, Ms. Chou began the lesson with a short large-group experience. She modeled how to read portions of the text aloud, using different voices for different speakers to demonstrate for students how to understand who was speaking, Cowgirl Kate or her horse.

She then met with smaller groups and modeled how to determine meanings of key terms through context clues. Her instruction was differentiated based on the instructional needs of the students. For example, with one group she modeled how to figure out words using illustrations as context clues as she explained that she understood the meaning of *saddlebags* because of the illustrations, which showed the horse sniffing the saddlebags. With another group, she modeled how surrounding words often can provide meanings for unknown words, showing how she inferred the meaning of *cowhorse* by looking at the two sentences that immediately followed this unknown word.

After working with each group, Ms. Chou asked students to work in pairs at their seats to read two pages of text, practicing the use of context clues to figure out new words. She guided all students with a text-dependent question: *What do the words the authors use tell you about the characters and their actions?* Students were encouraged to annotate the text, noting what words and phrases meant and how this information added to their overall understanding of the text.

By the third day of close reading, students understood how dialogue was used in the text and how to determine new word meanings by using context clues. At this point, Ms. Chou felt that students were ready to read for understanding of the setting. She directed students to work with a partner to reread the chapter a third time, circling clues and illustrations that provided evidence of where the story took place. As they did so, she met in small groups with students who were having difficulty, reading portions of the story aloud and modeling how to locate examples of evidence for the ranch setting. She then gave these students the opportunity to silently read one page on their own.

At the end of the session, she brought all the students together in a large group and invited them to share their text-based evidence of the story's setting. They did so, noting the textual references to pastures, herding cows, discussion of saddlebags, and cowhorses, as well as information from the illustrations that showed Kate in a cowboy hat, boots, a bandana, and so on. Ms. Chou created a semantic map on the board to synthesize all of the students' examples and to extend student thinking by asking them to identify other things they might see on a ranch.

As students gain skill in close reading, they can be engaged in a close reading across the disciplines, which provides additional opportunities to work the process into the school day. Knowledge of content and text structure will grow as they learn to closely read many sources, including textbooks, primary source documents, maps, charts and graphs, and math problems. Supporting student proficiency in the process ensures their confidence and independence. In Chapter 4, we will provide suggestions for teaching close reading across the disciplines.

Differentiating Close Reading

All students can learn to read closely, provided their teacher is able to differentiate instruction for those who need additional supports to effectively read complex text, such as English language learners and striving readers.

One approach is to use the Gradual Release of Responsibility (GRR) instructional framework (Fisher & Frey, 2014; Pearson & Gallagher, 1983). After the first independent close reading, you might model a strategy *(I do it)* as you read the text aloud, have students try out the strategy in a group rereading *(we do it together)*, have students practice that strategy with a partner in another pass *(you do it together)*, and then employ the strategy independently *(you do it alone)*.

Consider the approach taken by 1st grade teacher Abdi Daar, who conducted a close reading using an excerpt from the first chapter of *Mr. Popper's Penguins* (1992) by Richard and Florence Atwater. Mr. Daar chose this text because of the stretch it provided his students in terms of vocabulary and meaning (see the Qualitative Scoring Rubric for Narrative Text, Figure 1.2, p. 25). For this lesson, he introduced the title of the chapter, "Stillwater," projected an excerpt on the board for everyone to see, and passed out individual copies as he set the lesson purposes: "We're going to read this story to understand what kind of a character Mr. Popper is, and how we decided this." The students listened and followed along as he read the text aloud. After the initial shared reading, he invited them to individually annotate their copy of the text *(you do it alone)* as he read the five-paragraph excerpt again; this time he asked them to find words indicating what kind of person Mr. Popper was—words like *house painter, untidy,* and *dreamer*. He explained that their annotations could also take the form of quick sketches rather than highlighting, circling, or adding notes in the margin. Students shared their annotations first with a partner and then with the whole group. Mr. Daar reminded students to show evidence from the text when describing Mr. Popper.

Although Mr. Daar was doing the oral reading, he was asking the students to do the thinking on their own. An initial close reading involves students working alone before they partner share *(you do it together)*.

Before the next reading, Mr. Daar said to his students, "Now I will model for you what I can learn about Mr. Popper. I will read the first two paragraphs. Notice how I think aloud and how I annotate to help me make the text mine. You might want to circle and add notes to your paper as you watch me." This *I do it* stage is important, as it allows students to see the language and the thinking processes that are involved with comprehending difficult text. During this next reading, Mr. Daar attended to the title, thinking aloud about why an author would name the chapter "Stillwater" and how that might relate to the main character. He also highlighted the phrases *spattered here and there with paint* and *wallpaper clinging to his hair and whiskers*, thinking aloud about how they gave evidence for Mr. Popper's untidiness. Then he asked the students if they had learned anything new about Mr. Popper through the second reading. They shared these responses with the whole group.

During a third reading (*we do it together*), Mr. Daar read the next two paragraphs, asking students to take a closer look at the words and phrases the author used and make a note of those that provided more information about Mr. Popper. "What more do you know about Mr. Popper?" Mr. Daar asked. "After I read, please work with your partner to annotate other descriptions of Mr. Popper." Later, as partner pairs shared their annotations and ideas with the whole group, Mr. Daar asked text-dependent questions such as *What evidence from the text told us that Mr. Popper is a dreamer? How do we know Mr. Popper is absentminded? How does being a dreamer and being absentminded relate to one another? What does the last line cause you to conclude about Mr. Popper?* He ended this GRR/close reading lesson by asking groups of students to put all their notes and knowledge together to come up with a complete description of Mr. Popper (*you do it together*). He explained that they could share their descriptions in writing, through an oral presentation, or as an illustration.

With struggling or emergent readers, consider using fluency routines to scaffold close reading. For example, if your students are reading a complex stretch text excerpt from a text exemplar, after the first reading, you might ask your English language learners or striving readers to engage with the text by using paired repeated readings. This scaffold would support their fluency and very probably promote their comprehension, preparing them to participate in the whole-group discussion of the next reading. Or, if there are challenging academic terms in the text, you might have students work with a partner to create 4-Square Word Cards like the one shown in Figure 3.14. If the text has an unfamiliar structure, you can call students' attention to that structure through text-dependent questions that address it.

Differentiating instruction for English language learners should involve the use of oral language as part of every close reading experience. Partner talk can be invaluable for English learners as they grapple with challenging texts. They might share with a partner their initial impressions of the text, retell the text to a partner, or summarize key points from the text. The use of sentence frames can also facilitate this process.

Grouping Arrangements That Support Close Reading Instruction and Learning

Effective grouping patterns can help to ensure student success with the complex texts required for close reading. Over the course of the close reading experience, students should have large-group, small-group, paired, and individual learning arrangements.

Figure 3.14 | **A 4-Square Word Card to Scaffold Academic Vocabulary in Simon's _Horses_**

Target Word & Definition	Visual
Albino Having no color (adj)	
Synonym colorless	**Sentence** Because of their fur, albino rats can camouflage themselves into white flowers.

Courtesy of Kiera Loveless.

Here's an illustration that shows an approach taken by 3rd grade teacher Al Sanchez when he engaged his students, who were predominantly English language learners, in a close reading of an excerpt from the Common Core text exemplar _Bat Loves the Night: Read and Wonder_, an informational storybook "stretch text" (560L) by Nicola Davies.

Mr. Sanchez began the lesson by sharing with students that the purpose for reading this text was to learn about the habits of bats. During the first reading, students worked independently to read and annotate the text, focusing on main ideas, unknown vocabulary, and areas of confusion. During a large-group follow-up discussion of the text, Mr. Sanchez observed that many students were confused by the text's layout and its use of different fonts (the text combined a small, italicized font for key facts about bats with a larger and different font that told the actual story). During the next reading, students worked in pairs to closely analyze the text layout. Mr. Sanchez asked them to share with a partner why they thought the author chose to use the different fonts and how the author decided where to place the small-font "factoids." After a few minutes, he prompted the students to share their responses, which he recorded on the board, and then modeled for students how to read the text in view of these text features. After students read and reread the excerpt, they discussed what they had learned about the habits of bats. Next Mr. Sanchez assigned students to small writing groups and had them use multiple sources to create their own informational storybook on a topic of their choice using the format features of *Bat Loves the Night* as a mentor text. In total, he used four different grouping patterns during key phases of the lesson. Students worked individually during the first reading, discussed the text in a large group and worked in pairs during the next reading, and then gathered in small writing groups to create a similar text.

Self-Assessment, Reflection, and Next Steps

Consider using the self-assessment checklist shown in Figure 3.15 to reflect on both your current familiarity with text complexity and close reading and your current close reading implementation practices. This form might also be the centerpiece of the discussion of these topics in a professional learning community (PLC).

On your own or with the members of your PLC, use the checklist to reflect on what you understand about close reading and how you use text complexity and close reading strategies. Identify the aspects of close reading implementation you are doing effectively and those that are more problematic. Over time, the information you gather with this form can be helpful as an informal record of progress and may be useful in planning individual or schoolwide professional development experiences.

Finally, in **Appendix A: A Guide for Administrators,** we provide suggestions for how administrators can support whole-school implementation of close reading instruction, a Close Reading Observation Guide designed to parallel the Planning Guide for Close Reading shared in Figure 3.12, and resources administrators can consult to learn more and find information to share with teachers. By creating common understandings around the practice of close reading, administrators can better support teachers as they work to become proficient in this practice.

≡◈≡

As we have seen, in close reading, the teacher uses a combination of planning, structured implementation, and thoughtful management to set conditions under which students create their own deep knowledge and understanding of a text and an author's message. As teachers and students increase their familiarity with close reading practices, they will find that close reading promotes the kind of critical thinking essential to success in school and in the workplace. In the next chapter, we explore how teachers can move close reading beyond the boundaries of the language arts classroom and into disciplinary instruction.

Figure 3.15 | **Close Reading Expertise and Implementation Self-Assessment**

Download

TEACHER EXPERTISE	Beginning	Progressing	Accomplished
1. Am I aware of the kinds of texts that are appropriate for close reading?			
2. Do I understand the quantitative factors of text complexity?			
3. Do I understand the qualitative dimensions of text complexity?			
4. Can I identify reader/task features that influence text complexity?			
5. Can I evaluate a text for complexity based on quantitative, qualitative, and reader/task factors?			
6. Can I identify potential close reading teaching points based on my text and reader assessments?			
7. Do I understand the steps in close reading and how it differs from traditional reading instruction?			
8. Do I understand how to create effective text-dependent questions?			
CLOSE READING IMPLEMENTATION	**Beginning**	**Progressing**	**Accomplished**
1. Have I made close reading a part of my regular classroom schedule?			
2. Do I implement close reading in my classroom on a daily basis?			
3. Does close reading occur in content area subjects as well as language arts time?			
4. Do student close reading experiences incorporate the Gradual Release of Responsibility model?			
5. Do I use formative assessment to determine students needs and next steps for instruction during close reading?			
6. Do I differentiate instruction based on formative assessments as part of close reading experiences?			
7. Do I use a variety of grouping arrangements to support close reading instruction and learning?			

Based on a reflection of my knowledge of Close Reading practice, what are my next steps for professional development?

How do I plan to begin?

CHAPTER 4

READING CLOSELY ACROSS THE DISCIPLINES

One of the most radical changes of the Common Core State Standards is that they make literacy a critical part of instruction in all disciplines and at all grade levels. This is a departure from the No Child Left Behind era, where social studies and science instruction took a back seat to reading and mathematics. The literacy that the Common Core calls for is *disciplinary literacy*—that is, using reading, reasoning, investigating, speaking, and writing to develop content knowledge related to a particular discipline (McConachie & Petrosky, 2010). This embrace of disciplinary literacy is an acknowledgement of how central reading and writing are to the real-world work of historians, mathematicians, scientists, software engineers, and those in other technical disciplines. While science teachers, for example, may think of science as a hands-on pursuit, fully 50 percent of the work that scientists actually do involves reading (Hunt Institute, 2011).

Note that disciplinary literacy is not just another name for *content area literacy* (Shanahan & Shanahan, 2012). The latter focuses on generic strategies, such as questioning and summarizing, that students can use to boost general comprehension while reading textbooks in social studies, mathematics, science, and other classes. Disciplinary literacy, by contrast, includes specific literacy practices that disciplinary experts have identified as ones they use to make sense of information within their disciplines. These practices are not generic; they are unique to each area of study. For example, Shanahan and Shanahan (2008), studying the literacy practices engaged in by experts in the various disciplines, found that chemists read texts with the intent to study them more deeply through replication of the identified processes and tasks, while historians perceive texts as interpretations that often hold bias. The goal of disciplinary literacy instruction is to teach students to use these specific strategies, which are different for each discipline, as they read all kinds of texts within an area of study.

This chapter looks at reading and writing strategies that pertain to close reading across all of the content areas. While we use the terms *content areas* and *disciplines* interchangeably, the close reading and other literacy practices we discuss can be applied to all of the content areas rather than to the work done exclusively by scientists, historians, mathematicians, and rhetoricians. The development of these more generic literacy skills in grades K–5 supports the disciplinary literacy practices of students as they move into grades 6–12. We view close reading as a literacy practice that supports an analytic investigation of a text in any discipline and that, through the text-dependent questions being asked, can help students investigate texts in ways similar to how a disciplinary expert might interact with a text. In our discussion of close reading, we will share

- Ways to use multiple text types for close reading across the disciplines.
- The rationale for focusing on informational texts during close reading.
- How students build discipline-specific knowledge through experience with increasingly challenging texts.
- Resources for text exemplars and text sets for close reading in the disciplines.
- Examples of what close reading looks like in science, social studies, and mathematics.

Let's get started.

Why Reading Closely Across the Disciplines Is Essential

In close reading, students read and reread short complex texts—those that the teacher has identified as challenging based on evaluation of the text's structures and organization, language features, meaning, author's purpose, and knowledge demands. The students' purpose is to dig deeply into the content, focusing their attention on what's within the four corners of that text.

There are many reasons for close reading to be a component of all disciplinary learning and instruction. Here are three we find particularly compelling.

Embedded Disciplinary Literacy Instruction

The Common Core envisions literacy instruction as something that is embedded within the curriculum of all disciplines rather than something confined to "language arts time." The practice of close reading is an ideal means for achieving this kind of literacy integration. Through close reading, a teacher can increase the amount of reading students do in social studies, science, and other subjects and promote long-term retention of content-related information. Close reading also gives students practice mastering the "ways of knowing" that are pertinent to each discipline. For example, one important way of knowing that is characteristic of social studies is understanding how a text's author shapes the information he or she delivers. When historians read, they interpret a text by asking themselves who the author of that text is, what the author knows about a topic, and what the author's biases might be. If necessary, they analyze information in historical maps and charts and make connections among economics, religion, government, and cultural topics (Wineberg, 1991, 1998). So, for example, when 5th graders do a close reading of Sojourner Truth's "Ain't I a Woman" speech, the teacher can frame the experience in ways that require students to continually revisit the text and, in doing so, expand their understanding of the author, the times in which she lived, and her circumstances as they consider and reconsider the meaning of her message.

Opportunity to Acquire and Develop Discipline-Based Knowledge

The Common Core standards expect students to use reading experiences to build a coherent body of knowledge in the various disciplines as they move through the grades. As their knowledge in the discipline grows, so will their ability to grasp and assimilate the new ideas they will encounter in their reading. As Lee and Spratley (2010) remind us, "If you don't know content you will have a difficult time understanding the texts, and if you don't understand the texts you are unlikely to learn content" (p. 3). Ideally, daily close reading sessions should be structured so that each experience builds on the one before it so that students use text to build conceptual knowledge over time.

Teachers may want to collaborate with colleagues in and across grade levels to ensure an ever-expanding trajectory of challenge in their close reading texts within and across grade levels. For example, in 1st grade, students might read National Geographic's "Wind Power", a Common Core text exemplar listed in Appendix B of the ELA/literacy standards document (NGA Center & CCSSO, 2010b) that explores the movement of wind and its connection to temperature. Carefully crafted text-dependent questions would direct students to note the key elements of moving air. A few years later, in 4th grade, these students might closely read *Hurricanes: Earth's Mightiest Storms,* another Common Core text exemplar, which could kick off a deeper investigation of the relationship between the atmosphere and the ocean—a relationship that sometimes results in prime hurricane conditions that include high winds and rising air over warm oceans. So, in the primary grades, students would explore moving air in a general sense, and then in the intermediate grades, they would dig deeper to understand how air is affected by warm water.

Close reading experiences with disciplinary texts help students build their content knowledge over time through mastery of academic vocabulary, sensitivity to text structure, increased understanding of linguistic and discourse forms, and a developing understanding of authors' purposes. They push students to monitor their content comprehension as they reread to note key ideas; ask themselves questions about the content; visualize people, places, and events; and make predictions and connections among related topics. Students develop facility with close reading at different rates, and some may need more support than others. Fortunately, the skill development progression in the Common Core standards can help teachers identify the instructional interventions that each student needs.

Modeling of Disciplinary Literacy Practices

Close reading of disciplinary texts gives teachers a way to model for students how to address the unique comprehension challenges associated with particular content within a particular subject area. For example, elementary students can easily feel lost inside scientific texts, which lack the familiar beginning-middle-end structure of stories or other chronological narratives. What science texts tend to have are problem/solution or cause/effect text structures. By modeling how to look for and note these characteristic text structures while reading (e.g., pointing out key phrasings, such as *if . . . then* or *when . . . then* or *because . . .*), a teacher can clarify for students how science writing is put together. Science readers also need to know how to interpret information presented in charts or graphs and identify trends. An astute teacher will model how to notice the axes of a graph, including units, and then how to determine if a value is increasing or decreasing relative to another quantity. These are just two examples of disciplinary literacy skills that are rarely taught explicitly, yet are essential to comprehending science texts.

A teacher who models disciplinary literacy strategies within the context of close reading demonstrates for students how scientists, historians, mathematicians, and other professionals read and reread to unlock the deeper meanings found within complex texts. With these tools at their disposal, students are better prepared to engage with various disciplines' critical content, vocabulary, forms of discourse, and linguistic and text structures, and they are positioned to strengthen these skills with each new close reading experience. At the end of this chapter, we provide examples of how teachers use close reading to model learning across the disciplines.

Using Multiple Text Types in Disciplinary Close Reading

The Common Core State Standards make texts central to classroom instruction as never before. Consider that the word *text* represents 19 percent of the total words in the Common Core ELA/literacy standards document, compared to less than 1 percent of typical state standards documents (Burkins & Yaris, 2012). It's notable, too, that all the key instructional shifts that the Common Core requires (CCSSI, 2014) have a relation to texts.

Here is how the ELA/literacy standards document sums up the kind of reading students should do:

> Students must read widely and deeply from among a broad range of high-quality, increasingly challenging literary and informational texts. Through extensive reading of stories, dramas, poems, and myths from diverse cultures and different time periods, students gain literary and cultural knowledge as well as familiarity with various text structures and elements. By reading texts in history/social studies, science, and other disciplines, students build a foundation of knowledge in these fields that will also give them the background to be better readers in all disciplines. Students can only gain this foundation when the curriculum is intentionally and coherently structured to develop rich content knowledge within and across grades. (NGA Center & CCSSO, 2010a, p. 40)

Why is reading deeply and broadly so important? Because it translates into big improvements in student learning. Increasing the range and variety of texts increases reading competencies (Kuhn & Stahl, 2000) and improves achievement—not only in reading but in other content areas as well (Guthrie, Schafer, Von Secker,

& Alban, 2000). When is the last time your students read a play or a technical text in your classroom? The truth is, most teachers engage students with a pretty limited range of texts. Remembering that literacy knowledge comes from literacy experiences (Palincsar & Duke, 2004), if we want students to read and comprehend multiple text types, if we want them to reap the full benefits of close reading, they need exposure to lots of different texts and instruction on how to read these texts.

Even in the early grades, texts from the different disciplines are drastically different from one another, representing very different discourse forms. As Buell (2009) puts it, they represent "different worlds . . . different purposes, different writing styles, different organizations, different language, different modes of communication, different visual layouts, different expectations of relevant background and experiences, and different uses of knowledge" (p. 230).

Each genre has unique features, and reading comprehension is genre-dependent (Duke & Roberts, 2010). Genre-specific strategies help students understand the unique features of each text type. In other words, the reading processes needed to comprehend a science-based fictional story like Madeleine L'Engle's *A Wrinkle in Time* are different from those needed to extract information from a *National Geographic Kids* article like "Seeking the Stars." The texts themselves are written for different purposes, using different language. *A Wrinkle in Time* is written with attention to character description, emotive language, and story structure. "Seeking the Stars" is constructed using data, academic language, topical words, and quotes from science researchers. It makes sense that students would need explicit instruction in specific strategies unique to reading and writing in a particular genre if they are to successfully negotiate the many text types they should encounter as part of close reading.

One of the demands of the Common Core's writing standards is that students be capable of writing in three different genres: *narrative, informative/explanatory text,* and *persuasive text/argument* (which, in grades K–5, takes the form of students writing about their opinions). Through close reading experiences with each genre, students will gain experience with all three of these text types, and that will make writing in each genre easier. As you will see in Chapter 5, language and writing experiences can be closely aligned with close reading practices.

The Common Core ELA/literacy standards specifically mention and reference a wide range of genre examples across the K–5 grade span, and we'd like to take a closer look at them now. For discussion, we have divided the genres recommended and referenced in the standards into three categories: *literature, informational text,* and *additional forms.*

Literature

Literary study of stories, dramas, and poetry often occurs in the English language arts classroom, but it need not be confined to that discipline. Teachers of social studies, science, and technical subjects can also use these literary forms for close reading experiences. Selected text exemplar stories and poems can be grouped together as *text sets* to be used when studying a particular concept, era, theory, or theme. (Later in this chapter we will provide more information on text sets.)

In grades K–5, students are expected to spend 50 percent of their in-school reading time reading literature. Despite what some have suggested, the Common Core standards do not advocate the abandonment of literature study. They do, however, identify three types of literature—*stories, drama,* and *poetry*—that should account for most of the reading students will do in English language arts.

Stories are imaginative narratives that include characters, plots, and settings. Stories take many different forms, including the following text types:

- *Fables*—short tales containing a moral, like *Aesop's Fables.*
- *Fantasy*—highly imaginative fiction often containing magic and imaginary worlds. Fantasy books are extremely popular with children, and titles like J. K. Rowling's Harry Potter books are typical of the genre.
- *Folktales*—stories that have been passed down via oral tradition and retold over time.
- *Historical fiction*—stories with settings and some actual people from the historical past but with fictional or fictionalized main characters. For example, the text exemplar *Sarah, Plain and Tall,* by Patricia MacLachlan, is set in a time and place that actually existed, but all of the characters are fictional.
- *Myths*—stories that explain the mysteries of life and the world.
- *Legends*—traditional tales of a group, first told orally and later in written form, like the King Arthur stories.
- *Mysteries*—narratives that involves solving a crime or getting to the bottom of an unexplained event.
- *Adventure stories*—narratives that include unexpected and dangerous events. Joan Aiken's *The Wolves of Willoughby Chase* describes an ominous, imaginary time in England when the country was overrun by wolves. The two main

characters, Bonnie and Sylvia, encounter many obstacles as they escape their evil governess, survive a terrible orphanage, and ultimately return to their beloved home, Willoughby Chase.

Drama is the second type of literature noted in the Common Core. A drama is a play that contains one or more acts. It can be read or performed by actors, and is often captured on video or film. Many students enjoy the opportunity to perform in plays and take part in other drama-related classroom activities like Readers Theater.

Poetry is the third type of literary text. Poetry is a written form that uses sound, meaning, and rhythm to convey experience. The text exemplar poems in the Common Core range from whimsical to thought provoking, and include works such as Edward Lear's "The Owl and the Pussycat" and Grace Nichols's "They Were My People."

Informational Text

Informational text, also known as *explanatory* or *expository text*, is an umbrella classification for a wide range of nonfiction text types written to inform readers about all kinds of topics in science, social science, current events, the arts, and more.

Informational texts have a strong presence in the Common Core State Standards. A key recommendation of the Common Core is that elementary school students spend 50 percent of reading time focused on informational text, with that percentage increasing to 70 percent by the end of high school (NGA Center & CCSSO, 2010a). It is assumed that informational text will have a prominent place in the Common Core assessments being developed by Smarter Balanced and PARCC.

There are at least three justifications for the Common Core's emphasis on informational text. First, traditionally, students have had minimal exposure to informational genres in school. Nell Duke (2000) found that the 1st graders in the classrooms she studied spent on average only 3.6 minutes with informational text per day. The picture in grades 2, 3, and 4 is equally bleak. In a more recent study of 2nd through 4th graders' experiences with informational texts, students in 2nd grade got only one minute a day of exposure to informational text, while 3rd and 4th graders averaged only 16 minutes per day (Jeong, Gaffney, & Choi, 2010). Furthermore, basal readers expose students to a narrow range of informational text types (Moss, 2008), and children in preschool through 3rd grade seldom hear informational texts read aloud, whether at home or at school (Yopp & Yopp, 2006). If students are to read informational texts 50 percent of the time during the school day, as the Common Core standards require, they will need access to and experience with far more informational texts across all disciplines than are presently available.

The second justification for emphasizing informational text is that it is the favorite type of reading for many children. One of the authors of this book, Barbara, remembers a visit to a school in Canton, Ohio, where she met a boy named Brandon who was passionate about animals. According to Brandon's teacher, most books he read in and out of school were informational books about this topic. During Barbara's brief conversation with Brandon, he clutched a book titled *Animals of the Rain Forest* and explained with great seriousness his fascination with it: "I like information. Stories just tell you something silly, like bears with clothes on. This gives more information than stories. It makes you smarter. Everything you think about is in this book" (Moss, 2002b, p. 37).

Informational texts have great power to engage young children in learning about the real world. Through this engagement, they increase their content knowledge, academic vocabulary, and understanding of informational discourse. At the same time, they develop the love of reading so critical to creating lifelong readers.

A third and final justification for emphasizing informational text is that school and workplace success depends on the ability to read it. According to Kamil (2004), "Nothing is more important to a student's success in school than the ability to read and write expository text." Furthermore, the literacy demands of today's technological society require that students be able to read and write the largely expository text that appears on Internet websites (Kamil & Lane, 1997). As Pearson (2004) notes, "it is competence with expository reading, not narrative reading, that most concerns educators and future employers" (p. 222).

Think about the reading you do every day. You may read a newspaper, the various e-mail messages in your inbox, your students' social studies text, notes from parents, online news stories and interviews, part of a novel, or a few articles in a favorite magazine. We read online and offline, and we encounter a multiplicity of text types—some narrative, but a lot more informational. If we are to adequately prepare students for college or the workplace, we need to give them the tools they need to succeed when reading informational texts.

Informational texts are the second major category represented in the Common Core State Standards. As noted, they encompass a broad range of texts. Just as stories include realistic fiction, historical fiction, adventure stories, mystery stories, fantasies, and other forms, informational texts range from biographies, which are often written more like stories, to functional texts, like bus schedules and directions for downloading apps. Many teachers involve students in the study of biography, but this is just one type of the many kinds of informational text that students need to encounter. The Common Core identifies four specific categories of informational texts: *literary nonfiction, expository text, argument* (or persuasion); and *procedural texts.* Students should experience each of these types of texts in close reading experiences.

Literary nonfiction refers to texts that present factual information but use a narrative format, including narrative devices like metaphors, similes, and dialogue. It usually has a clear beginning, middle, and end, and it combines narrative elements, like characters and plots, with informational ones (Duke & Bennett-Armistead, 2003). Literary nonfiction is designed so that readers will gain both enjoyment and information and will learn to appreciate the author's craft in terms of word choice, phrases, and structural elements. Many books for younger readers fit into this category, as the narrative aspects of the text act as a bridge to the information it provides.

Literary nonfiction includes the following text types:

- *Biography*—an account of a person's life written by another. The text exemplar *Lincoln: A Photobiography* by Russell Freedman is a Newbery-winning account of the life of the 16th president of the United States that acknowledges his many accomplishments but also reveals him as a human being with weaknesses.
- *Autobiography*—a full account of a person's life so far, written by the person himself or herself.
- *Personal memoir*—an account of a specific period in a person's life written by the person himself or herself. A personal memoir is distinguished from an autobiography by its focus on a more limited time frame and the writer's experiences during that particular time.

The K–1 informational storybook text exemplar *Starfish,* by Edith Thacher Hurd, is a good example of literary nonfiction. While it provides information about starfish and their habitats, body parts, and behaviors, that information is conveyed in descriptive language (*it slides and it glides on its tiny tube feet*) rather than in straight, factual exposition.

Expository texts include informational trade books, textbooks, news articles, feature articles, encyclopedia entries, and historical documents. They are generally structured using patterns like description, sequence, causation, problem/solution, and comparison/contrast. They sometimes use signal words that denote the text structure, are written in third person (e.g., *There are three layers of the rain forest*), and use rhetorical structures like examples and repetition along with text features like subheadings, captions, sidebars, photos, and charts and tables. They often include visual features like maps, graphs, and charts.

Expository text types include the following:

- *Informative/explanatory texts*—texts written to convey information through exposition
- *Textbooks*—wide-ranging books providing information related to a discipline of study (e.g., chemistry, world history)
- *Encyclopedia entries*—articles that provide information pertaining to the entry's name
- *Historical documents*—texts that preserve and describe the records of a government, nation, or society
- *Visual texts*—maps, charts, graphs, political cartoons, or other documents that use images to convey information.

Gail Gibbons's *Nature's Green Umbrella: Tropical Rain Forests* is an expository picture book that provides the reader with information about rain forests. Describing where rain forests are found, the layers of a rain forest, and different kinds of rain forests, it is replete with maps, labeled diagrams, charts, and other visual text features. Expository texts are sometimes, but not always, less engaging than literary fiction; they focus mainly on straight factual information.

Functional/procedural texts provide instructions on how to complete a task. They show steps in a process or combine words and graphic elements to communicate the process to readers. Close readings of procedural texts on topics like how to use a search engine, how to do an online library search, or how to complete a craft activity combine practice in reading procedural texts with practical student needs and interests.

Procedural text types include the following:

- *Recipes*—instructions for making a particular dish (e.g., pizza).
- *Technical texts*—information and directions about how to perform a particular task (e.g., hang a light fixture).

- *Science experiments*—directions for how to carry out a specific investigation.
- *Manuals*—instructions about how to operate things, such as a computer or a cell phone.

Experiments and recipes are popular kinds of procedural texts; the K–1 read-aloud text exemplar *From Seed to Pumpkin* by Wendy Pfeffer contains a recipe for roasted pumpkin seeds and an experiment examining how plants drink water. Functional/procedural texts are quite suitable for close reading experiences for elementary students.

Persuasive and argumentative texts employ appeals designed to persuade an audience to the author's point of view. These can include appeals to reason or evidence, to audience needs or desires, or to the writer's credibility (Duke, Caughlan, Juzwik, & Martin, 2011). The teaching of argument is central to the Common Core standards, and the groundwork is laid in grades K–5, where students focus on analyzing and expressing opinion. This genre includes the following text types:

- *Opinion pieces*—texts in which the author take a position on an issue and argues its merits.
- *Advertisements*—promotional communications used in marketing to alert and persuade consumers.
- *Editorials*—articles written by an editor that state and support an opinion about a particular topic of public interest.
- *Persuasive letters*—texts in letter format that take a position and support it with evidence.
- *Letters to the editor*—letters to a newspaper or magazine editor expressing the author's beliefs regarding a particular topic of public interest.
- *Reviews*—critical pieces in which the author expresses and supports an opinion about the merit or content of a movie, book, play, piece of music, game, restaurant, product, or the like.
- *Brochures/flyers*—deliberately biased descriptions or advertisements in which the author works to persuade a reader to take action.

In the elementary grades, texts that use evidence to persuade the reader to a particular position can provide rich models for the kind of writing students will be doing once they reach middle school. For young children, a title like Amy Houts's *Let's Exercise!* presents simple arguments for the need for exercise. In the intermediate elementary grades, a book like Mary Miche's *Nature's Patchwork Quilt: Understanding Habitats* persuades readers of the reasons people need to work collaboratively to preserve biodiversity.

To start developing students' ability to express their opinion, teachers in the primary grades can engage students in a close reading/listening of Common Core text exemplars like Arnold Lobel's *Frog and Toad Together*. With this specific text, a teacher might ask students to identify the character they felt was the better friend. Then, the teacher can invite students to return to the text to find examples that support their opinions about which character is the better friend. Responses can be shared orally and in writing. Another text that could be used with 2nd or 3rd grade students to get them started with opinion writing as preparation for future argumentative writing is the Common Core text exemplar poem "Stopping by Woods on a Snowy Evening" by Robert Frost. Students might be asked to visit the text once to identify the theme and then read it again to find evidence that supports their opinion on the theme.

Other Text Forms

There are many other kinds of texts that are not easily classified because they are distinguished more by form than by content:

- *Graphic texts/novels*
- *Audio texts,* including podcasts, audiobooks, radio programs, and other audio-only formats.
- *Video texts,* including films, videos, and other visual formats.
- *Multimedia texts*, combining audio, still images, video, animation and other forms.
- *Digital texts,* which include blog posts or online discussions and electronic versions of written texts that students can access online or download onto tablets or other electronic devices.

Note that all of the content of the text types listed here can fall into any genre: fiction, nonfiction, fantasy, opinion pieces, reviews, and so on.

Digital texts merit a closer look, because when today's students are not in school, a lot of what they read is digital text. The Common Core acknowledges the need for students to read more of these digital texts in school—specifically online texts. The text exemplars even include some online texts. Furthermore, the Common Core assessments being developed by Smarter Balanced and

PARCC will be administered online, necessitating that students have experience reading these text types in a classroom setting.

Although the research on online comprehension is relatively new, it does suggest that online and offline reading comprehension are not the same, and that children require different comprehension skills and strategies in order to read effectively online. Consider these findings:

1. When children are reading online, the skills of locating and critically evaluating information are extremely important (Zawilinski & Leu, 2008).

2. Students may need specific instruction in online reading comprehension skills before they can successfully comprehend online texts (Leu et al., 2005). For example, students must know how to use search engines effectively in order to locate websites appropriate to their area of investigation. Similarly, students need to be taught to evaluate the "truth value" of the information they find online in order to assess its value and integrity.

3. A comparison of results on a standard statewide reading comprehension assessment and an online reading comprehension test showed that some students who performed poorly on the print assessment were among the highest performers on the digital version (Leu et al., 2005). This finding supports the claim that print reading comprehension and digital reading comprehension are different things.

The National Geographic Young Explorers online text *Garden Helpers* is a K–1 text exemplar appropriate for close reading with younger children. The teacher might focus on the author's purpose, the text structure, key vocabulary, and so on. In this particular visually appealing online text, readers hear the text read aloud and are simultaneously able to view photographs of the images that the text describes. As is typical in science texts, readers must shift their attention among various images, graphs, charts, data, and actual words. In this example, attention to the details of the images is essential to full comprehension. When the reader hears "An egret hops on a hippo. It eats bugs on the hippo. So the hippo stays healthy," she must identify what kind of animal an egret is by looking at the photo.

Close reading of *Garden Helpers* allows a teacher to effectively address a number of overarching science concepts. For instance, there are several passages providing detailed examples of bugs that help a garden flourish. There is also a section on the growth and maturation of corn, from seed to ear. Finally, there is a section about animals that help each other in symbiotic relationships.

In addition, a teacher using this text could focus on two specific aspects of online reading present in this text: clicking on a mouse to "turn the pages," and clicking on the sound icon to hear the text read aloud. By embedding instruction related to using online texts, you can help students develop the online comprehension skills they will need to succeed in the classrooms and workplaces of the future.

Text Exemplars: A Powerful Resource for Close Reading

So where can teachers find examples of the various types of texts? We recommend the text exemplars provided in Appendix B of the ELA/literacy standards document (NGA Center & CCSSO, 2010b). We've referred to them already, but it's important to take a moment to review why the text exemplars are such a great resource for busy teachers. The exemplars, online at www.corestandards.org/assets/ Appendix_B.pdf,* are a list of (and a collection of extracts from) narrative and informational texts arranged in grade-level bands (K–1, 2–3, 4–5), offered to give teachers representative examples of the kinds of complex texts appropriate for classroom use. They include fiction, informational text, and poetry that can be read aloud and read by students independently. In Appendix B of the standards document, the exemplars are explained as follows:

> The text samples primarily serve to exemplify the level of complexity
> and quality that the Standards require all students in a given grade band
> to engage with. Additionally, they suggest the breadth of texts that students should encounter in the text types required by the Standards. The
> choices should serve as useful guideposts in helping educators select texts
> of similar complexity, quality and range for their own classrooms. They
> expressly do not represent a partial or complete reading list. (NGA Center
> & CCSSO, 2010b, p. 2)

According the ELA/literacy standards document, these texts were chosen by a work group who took recommendations from teachers, educational leaders, and researchers who had used the titles successfully with children at the specified grade levels.

You are probably wondering how the texts recommended for use with the Common Core are different from the texts you use now. First, the texts recommended may represent a broader range of genres than you may be using in your

---

* Our own Appendix B, beginning on page 182, can help you locate the text exemplars we mention in this book within the standards document.

classroom, whether in a core reading program or in disciplinary textbooks. By specifying titles in seldom-taught genres like literary nonfiction and informational texts, the Common Core elevates these genres to a more prominent place in the hope that they will get more attention in classrooms. For example, Steve Otfinoski's *The Kid's Guide to Money: Earning It, Saving It, Spending It, Growing It, Sharing It* provides a kid-friendly introduction to economics that teaches students how to make money, invest money, and use credit cards responsibly. It provides depth on a topic that is critically important to real life but gets little attention in textbooks.

Second, the exemplar texts include more classic works than you may currently be teaching. For example, of the 10 stories listed for grades 4–5, five are canonical classics: *Alice's Adventures in Wonderland, The Secret Garden, The Black Stallion, The Little Prince,* and *Tuck Everlasting.*

The third and most dramatic difference between the materials you probably use now and those on the text exemplar list is the level of text complexity at particular grade bands (it's important to keep in mind that these are the identified levels to be mastered by the end of the school year). The titles you now teach at your grade level may appear at earlier grade levels on the text exemplar list. For example, *Sarah, Plain and Tall*, with a Lexile measure of 560L, is often taught in grade 4, but it is a text exemplar for the grades 2–3 band. Joy Hakim's *A History of US: Liberty for All? 1820–1860*, which is a common supplemental textbook for 8th grade American history, appears as a text exemplar at the grades 4–5 band. Poetry titles for grades 4–5, while not evaluated by Lexiles, include Robert Frost's "Stopping by Woods on a Snowy Evening," a selection with complex themes typically reserved for older students. The complexity of these texts suggests that students will need to grapple with them through close reading in order to understand them. As we illustrate in the scenarios in Chapter 6, many students who at first do not succeed when reading a particular complex text may need to be engaged in subsequent small-group instruction that prepares them to return for a later, *successful* read of the text.

Recommended Text Exemplars for Disciplinary Literacy

Teacher responses to the text exemplars are often, "But these are so hard! How can our students read these books?" Carol Jago makes an important point: "In our effort to provide students with readings that they can relate to, we sometimes end up teaching works that students can read on their own [instead] of teaching more worthwhile texts that they most certainly need assistance negotiating. . . . Classroom texts should pose intellectual challenges for readers and invite them to stretch and grow" (Common Core, 2012, pp. viii–ix). She correctly notes that students will need teacher assistance in negotiating these complex texts, especially in terms of background knowledge and vocabulary expertise requisite for both text-explicit and text-implicit comprehension.

The books listed in Figure 4.1 are texts from a variety of genres appropriate for different grade levels. Those that are Common Core exemplar texts are denoted with a asterisk. All are written by quality authors of different genres, and all are worth reading. We hope that the informational titles recommended may prompt those of you who generally stick to the textbook during social studies, mathematics, and science instruction to explore other reading materials, including primary source documents and online articles.

Figure 4.1 | **Text Exemplars and Recommended Titles for Close Reading in Various Disciplines**

Grade Level	Language Arts	Social Science	Mathematics	Science
K–1	*Little Bear** *"By Myself"* (poem)* *A Story: A Story**	*Family Pictures** *Tomas and the Library Lady**	*100 Days of School* *The Doorbell Rang* *Each Orange Had 8 Slices*	*Starfish** *Earthworms** *Water, Water Everywhere**
2–3	*Poppleton in Winter** *Henry and Mudge: The First Book of Their Adventures** *Tops & Bottoms**	*If the World Were a Village: A Book About the World's People** *Martin Luther King and the March on Washington** *The Story of Ruby Bridges**	*Sir Cumference and the First Round Table* *Math Curse* *The Greedy Triangle*	*"Fireflies"* (poem)* *Bats: Creatures of the Night** *Moonshot**
4–5	*Bud, Not Buddy** *M.C. Higgins, the Great** *Tuck Everlasting**	*The Birchbark House** *"The New Colossus"* (poem)* *My Librarian Is a Camel: How Books are Brought to Children Around the World**	*The Librarian Who Measured the Earth* *The Kid's Guide to Money: Earning It, Saving It, Spending It, Growing It, Sharing It** *Math Talk: Mathematical Ideas in Poems for Two Voices*	*Volcanoes** *Hurricanes: Earth's Mightiest Storms** *Quest for the Tree Kangaroo: An Expedition into the Cloud Forest of New Guinea**

*Common Core text exemplars

Text Sets for Close Reading in the Disciplines

Text sets are multigenre sets of books related to a single theme or essential question, and in the Common Core era, with standards stressing the importance of student experiences across texts rather than just within a single text, they are tremendously useful. Many teachers have already discovered the power of linking books together in ways that let students explore different aspects of a time period, topic, or experience. As Gay Ivey (2010) puts it, "[Students] can't learn much from just one book. . . . What we really want students to be able to do is read across text critically and analytically. We have become overly concerned with whether students can comprehend a particular text and not concerned enough about whether students can use multiple texts or grapple with big ideas" (p. 22).

Close reading of excerpts of books in text sets can engage students with important concepts that span more than one text. By seeing the same topic through multiple lenses, students expand their viewpoints, gaining exposure to voices that are often silenced. Guided by text-dependent questions, students can examine, compare, and analyze aspects of these texts in a way that leads to in-depth reflection on big ideas. These texts are also an excellent source for student independent reading on a content-related topic (Moss, 2011).

During a 3rd grade unit on crossing borders, for example, students could explore the experiences of immigrants through Jane Medina's *My Name is Jorge on Both Sides of the River*, a book of poems about a young Mexican boy learning about life in America; Helen Foster James and Virginia Shin-Mui Loh's *Paper Son*, the story of a young Chinese boy who emigrated to America alone through Angel Island; and Carol Bierman's *Journey to Ellis Island*, the true story of an 11-year-old Russian Jewish boy's trip to America through Ellis Island in the early 1900s. These three titles, representing the genres of poetry, historical fiction, and biography, provide students with different perspectives on the immigrant experience, including that of a modern immigrant child, a Chinese immigrant "paper son" who must pretend to be the son of a Chinese family in San Francisco in order to enter the country, and a Russian Jewish boy whose family has experienced hunger, poverty, and war in their native land. Through a Jigsaw instructional activity, students could share what they learned about the circumstances and experiences of each child. They could also compare the information provided in these texts with that found in their textbook on the topic of immigration, and in doing so, address a Common Core standard focused on integration of knowledge and ideas: "Compare and contrast the most important points and key details presented in two texts on the same topic" (RI.3.9).

Additional resources for text sets include the following:

- The *Common Core Curriculum Maps: English Language Arts, Grades K–5* (Common Core, 2012) contain sample thematic units that incorporate lists of texts representing classic and contemporary literature, readings on science and social science topics, and texts related to the arts and music. Sample unit titles include The Amazing Animal World, The Wild West, and Fantastic Adventures with Dragons, Gods, and Giants.

- Room for Debate (www.nytimes.com/roomfordebate) is a *New York Times* blog in which different arguments about issues or news events are discussed by four or six contributors. Each response is only four or five paragraphs, making this a great resource for close reading for upper elementary students. Topical issues include "Do we still need libraries?" and "Is organic food worth the expense?"

- The Teachers College Reading and Writing Project (http://readingandwritingproject.com) contains many text set resources for teachers. Its collection of digital science text sets and digital nonfiction text sets related to popular culture, science, and social studies can be particularly helpful.

Close Reading in Science, Social Studies, and Mathematics

In this section, we share examples of what is involved when engaging students in a close reading in some non-ELA disciplines, focusing on how to address both content learning requirements and standards and incorporate the reading of informational text in compliance with the Common Core. Be sure to take note of the text type used in each example and the specific instruction that is customized to the discipline.

Close Reading in Science

In science, the Common Core can be interpreted through a lens of inquiry, investigation, and problem solving, which are foundational elements of the Next Generation Science Standards and of any well-constructed science curriculum. Even 1st graders are now expected to plan and carry out investigations, construct explanations, and design solutions (Achieve et al., 2013). Clearly, such tasks cannot be accomplished without background knowledge built through informational reading.

Consider Common Core Reading Informational Text Standard 8, which focuses on evaluating arguments. The kindergarten-level version of this anchor standard states, "With prompting and support, identify the reasons an author gives to support points in a text" (RI.K.8). When scientists read information, they naturally look for supporting pieces of evidence that advance an idea or theory. When students are taught to identify the author's supporting points, they are seeking to identify evidence that can be later applied to a design project or a laboratory investigation. A close reading of an informational science text (e.g., a journal article, a firsthand account of a natural event, or a news story documenting recent research) offered with appropriate text-dependent questions can further a mindset that questions, predicts, designs, and investigates. Science readers read to determine credible evidence. They evaluate data. They interpret graphs and charts. And they draw conclusions.

By 2nd grade, students are expected to "Describe how reasons support specific points the author makes in a text" (RI.2.8). At this grade level, the standard asks that students delve deeply to connect text reasoning to author points, and to accomplish this, they will need multiple readings.

Consider the nonfiction text *Where Do Polar Bears Live?* The author, Sarah L. Thomson, describes characteristics of polar bears, emphasizing those qualities that allow them to live in their extreme Arctic environment, which she also describes. Finally, the author discusses how a cub will grow and develop. Given this range of topics, connected as they are, the teacher might focus students' first reading on simply getting the gist of text—gleaning its main ideas (e.g., this is a text about polar bears, the Arctic, cold weather). Then, to help students grasp the more sophisticated nuances of this interrelated text, the teacher might use text-dependent questions that guide students to find the author's descriptions of the cub at different stages: *He was no bigger than a guinea pig. Blind and helpless* and *Now it is spring—even though snow still covers the land* and *The cub is about the size of a cocker spaniel.* This kind of text evidence can help readers see that the author is discussing cub development in a harsh environment.

By 4th grade, Reading Informational Text Standard 8 expects students to "Explain how an author uses reasons and evidence to support particular points in a text" (RI.4.8). At this point, a teacher might have students do a first reading to determine the general sense of the text, a second reading to focus on a data table to determine trends, and a third reading to evaluate the study that generated the data as a way to evaluate the data's credibility. All these pieces of text evidence would work together to support a particular author point.

Reading a science text is clearly different than reading a historical account or a short story. It involves the mental accumulation of evidence and the simultaneous collection of data represented in graphic form, included as a support to the written text. Science readers commonly go back and forth between a graph and a part of the text to determine correlations and connections. They identify scales on graphs and charts. They determine cause/effect relationships. They look for patterns in data. They interpret models that represent real-world phenomena. And they identify and investigate systems. All these elements show up in science texts, and the expert reader must know how to discern them and how to interpret them. Close reading provides the instructional means to develop these skills.

Close Reading in the Social Sciences

The Common Core standards do not provide a blueprint for social studies instruction in grades K–5, but they do offer some clues about what social studies instruction that addresses the standards might look like. As Shennan Hutten (2013) observes, "The Common Core standards emphasize thinking skills, primary sources, evidence, analysis, point of view or perspective, and argument. These are not merely, or even primarily, English/Language Arts skills. They are closely related to historical inquiry, a process of helping students to act as historians" (p. 6).

Close reading in social science classes will look different from close reading in language arts classes in terms of (1) the types of complex texts used, (2) the instructional purposes, and (3) the teaching points addressed. Informational texts should represent 50 percent of students' reading experiences across the school day, and social studies is a logical place to include those texts. Starting in 2nd grade, the Common Core standards specifically require that students read, comprehend, and analyze complex informational and historical texts. They specifically mention informational text types appropriate for social studies—biography, autobiography, literary nonfiction, expository texts, and historical documents, which can include primary sources. From 2nd grade on, the standards also require that students interpret visual texts, either print or digital, like photographs, maps, graphs, and charts. These, too, are common resources in social studies. Therefore, close reading in social studies will include visual texts as well as print texts. For example, students might begin to experience close reading by exploring primary source photographs in 2nd grade, moving up to more sophisticated print and visual primary sources as they move through the grades. A 5th grade teacher might engage students in a close reading of a visual text, the famous political cartoon "Join or Die," considered the first political cartoon in America and attributed to Benjamin Franklin (see www.loc.gov/pictures/item/2002695523/). During the first encounter with the text, the teacher might ask students what they notice about this visual. Upon revisiting the text, the teacher might ask students to provide evidence that the cartoon is a map and identify which colonies were included on the map. On the third examination of the text, students could discuss in pairs the meaning of the caption "Join, or Die" and complete a quick-write about why Franklin might have published this particular cartoon and what he hoped to achieve through its publication.

The Common Core has also triggered a shift in the instructional objectives for close reading lessons in social studies. As early as grade 2, the reading standards for informational text require students to "describe the connection between a series of historical events" (RI.2.3). In grade 3, they must "describe the relationship between a series of historical events" (RI.3.3), and by grade 4, they must "explain events, procedures, ideas, or concepts in a historical . . . text, including what happened and why, based on specific information in the text" (RI.4.3). As you can see, this anchor standard requires progressively more critical thinking as students advance from grade to grade. Fourth graders must also "compare and contrast a firsthand and secondhand account of the same event or topic; describe the differences in focus and the information provided" (RI.4.6). To address this standard, 4th graders could compare the account of the experiences of the miners found in Rosalyn Schanzer's graphic text *Gold Fever! Tales from the California Gold Rush* with a primary source account of the experience—an excerpt from a letter written by Sheldon Shufelt to his cousin in 1850 (see www.eyewitnesstohistory.com/californiagoldrush.htm). The personal nature of Shufelt's letter, the many specific details about his life as a miner, and his specific voice create a clear contrast to the depiction of the Gold Rush miners in the secondary-source children's book.

Close Reading in Mathematics

Often in a math class, students must read exemplar problems or textbook explanations loaded with technical language, symbols, and concise, to-the-point sentences. Bear in mind, too, that the Common Core State Standards for Mathematics focus on specific skills at each grade-level band (e.g., students in grades K–2 study concepts, skill, and problem solving related to addition and subtraction; students in grades 3–5 look at multiplication and division of whole numbers and fractions). How can we merge the demands of content math learning with the focus on reading informational text called for by both sets of Common Core standards—math and ELA/literacy?

The intersection of these two areas of instructional need are math texts that include problem-solving information and data in real-world contexts. When students encounter texts that introduce a math-related concept (e.g., the number of animals on the endangered species list) or math word problems that ask them to do things like add the number of students buying apples to the number of students buying oranges at the market, some feel overwhelmed by the mix of numerals and words. As one 3rd grader told us, "When there are numbers in sentences, I get confused." A close reading with well-crafted text-dependent questions can help focus students by directing their thinking, in a progressive manner, to the appropriate parts of the text that provide clues to math problem solving or data/number analysis.

Although the kinds of problems that students will solve in a math class may differ in length and in subsequent task from a math-related informational text that connects math to the real world, many of the skills needed for both tasks could be taught through a close reading. Consider this paragraph from a *Time* magazine article called "Families: Pulling the Plug on TV" (Cornell, 2000):

> Fun isn't the only benefit of going TV-less. Television gobbles up 40 percent of Americans' free time. Doing without TV allows people to do lots of positive things. More than 80 percent of nearly 500 children in the survey play sports. Four-fifths of TV-free children have above-average reading skills: 41 percent read an hour or more a day. Nine of 10 families eat dinner together at least four times a week. Overall, they average nearly an hour a day of meaningful conversation. "It seems like such a simple solution," says Brock.

Notice how the text is strewn with numbers—percentages, raw numbers, and ratios. To glean meaning from this data, a reader must negotiate both phrase meaning and numerical data. It is a skill that is characteristic of math reading—and something that adept math readers do seamlessly. A student engaging in a first reading of this text would undoubtedly garner a general understanding that the text is about the effects of turning off the TV. A second reading might be focused by a text-dependent question that asks the reader what math terms or ideas the author uses to provide evidence for the claim being made. A third reading could involve a response to a text-dependent question that homes in on assessment of a claim (e.g., "What do you think of the data the author provides to support her claim?"). With each subsequent reading, the student goes deeper, considering the statistics, the claim, and the value of the numbers.

⇒◆⇐

Through close reading experiences in all of the disciplines, students will develop the skills they need to effectively master the wide array of disciplinary literacy skills they will need to succeed in college or the workplace. With the help of effective teachers, student mastery of these skills can become a reality. In Chapter 5, we use scenarios to illustrate some of the speaking, listening, and writing practices that these teachers so naturally apply to close reading practice.

CHAPTER 5

SUPPORTING ACADEMIC COMMUNICATION ABOUT CLOSELY READ TEXTS

There is power in having the language you need to communicate your ideas effectively. In her memoir, United State Supreme Court Justice Sonia Sotomayor notes that facility with language provides the self-confidence necessary to converse with a wide array of people across many situations: "It occurred to me that if I was going to be a lawyer—or, who knows, a judge—I had to learn to speak persuasively and confidently in front of an audience. I couldn't be a quivering mess of nerves" (2013, p. 85).

Developing this facility with language takes time. For some students, opportunities to engage in meaningful conversation around myriad topics begin long before kindergarten (Hart & Risley, 1995). Children of college-educated parents often have an advantage here. Their home language experiences, which support the development of vocabulary and the skillful use of language, prosody, syntax, grammar, and rules of conversation, provide the foundation for academic success. It is therefore not surprising that so many of the Common Core's ELA/literacy standards address students' use of language—in speaking, in listening, and in writing—with the intent that all students, and especially English language learners, receive enhanced language opportunities.

As the introduction to the ELA/literacy standards document notes, students acquire language proficiency across the disciplines as they "read purposefully and listen attentively to gain both general knowledge and discipline-specific expertise. They refine and share their knowledge through writing and speaking" (NGA Center & CCSSO, 2010a, p. 7). Although the individual's interaction with the text is an essential process of close reading, the ability to communicate about what is read is a major component of it as well. Being able to succeed with text investigations and collaborate effectively during a close reading encounter develops the language functions of speaking, listening, and writing. In turn, being able to read, discuss, and then write about a text facilitates deeper understanding of the information and language that text contains.

If we expect students to communicate about the texts they are reading, we must teach them how to do so. To become proficient communicators, students need supported practice speaking and writing about all kinds of topics in the disciplines of mathematics, science, art, literature, social studies, and technical subjects; it must be a significant component of instruction. In this chapter, we focus on various ways to provide students with opportunities to communicate about a text before they begin a close reading, throughout the close reading, and as they collaborate and share ideas through oral and written discourse after a close reading. While there are multiple standards identified within each ELA/literacy strand of the Common Core, we will address only those that pertain to communication relevant to a close reading.

Language for Speaking and Listening

The Common Core ELA/literacy standards contain a strand focused on speaking and listening and a strand focused on language. While speaking and language are obviously related, each has distinct features. Speaking involves verbally communicating through (1) *language*, which has vocabulary and rules related to grammar, syntax, and use (register), and (2) *pragmatics*, which involves the context and relationship of speaker and listener. Martin Joos (1967) identifies five language registers—styles of using language—that people employ during various language-based interactions:

- *Frozen register*—language that remains fixed, such as the Lord's Prayer
- *Formal or academic register*—language used for "proper" public speaking and classroom talk or discourse
- *Consultative register*—language used to ask for assistance from a supervisor or employer
- *Casual (informal) register*—language used when talking with friends or family in a casual setting
- *Intimate register*—language shared privately in love relationships.

"Language power" comes from knowing when and with whom to use each register. Speaking, listening, and language unite as speakers attempt to convey a verbal message within each register. The more proficient students are at using the formal or academic register of a language, the better they will be at both retrieving information during a close reading and conveying information through speaking and writing so that it will be understood by the listener or the reader.

Clearly, the question is how to help students develop the language power they need to communicate effectively in close reading sessions. Before discussing instructional practices that support language development for close reading, though, let's first consider the Common Core's anchor standards for both language and speaking and listening. The outcomes they aim for are closely related when it comes to communicating about texts verbally and in writing.

The Common Core's Language Standards

There are six Common Core language anchor standards organized under three headings.

Conventions of Standard English

CCRA.L.1. Demonstrate command of the conventions of standard English grammar and usage when writing or speaking.

CCRA.L.2. Demonstrate command of the conventions of standard English capitalization, punctuation, and spelling when writing.

Language Standards 1 and 2 emphasize knowing the conventions of grammar, punctuation, and spelling, and when and how to use these skills in creating a text. This kind of competence is essential during text annotation, collaborative conversations, and the writing that students do during and after a close reading. The reference to "standard English" indicates that speakers must be prepared to address a wider audience than their casual register may allow. Both of these standards remind us of how significantly students' language proficiency or the lack thereof affects their school experiences.

Knowledge of Language

CCRA.L.3. Apply knowledge of language to understand how language functions in different contexts, to make effective choices for meaning or style, and to comprehend more fully when reading or listening.

Language Standard 3, first addressed in 2nd grade, relates to close reading because the process requires students to grapple with language in various contexts, including the different genres of texts and registers students use to talk and write about them.

Vocabulary Acquisition and Use

CCRA.L.4. Determine or clarify the meaning of unknown and multiple-meaning words and phrases by using context clues, analyzing meaningful word parts, and consulting general and specialized reference materials, as appropriate.

CCRA.L.5. Demonstrate understanding of figurative language, word relationships, and nuances in word meanings.

CCRA.L.6. Acquire and use accurately a range of general academic and domain-specific words and phrases sufficient for reading, writing, speaking, and listening at the college and career readiness level; demonstrate independence in gathering vocabulary knowledge when encountering an unknown term important to comprehension or expression.

The three anchor standards under this heading illustrate the precision with language students need to be able to select just the right words to convey ideas during a collaborative conversation or to generate writing in response to information gleaned during close reading.

The Common Core's Speaking and Listening Standards

There are six Common Core speaking and listening anchor standards organized under two headings.

Comprehension and Collaboration

CCRA.SL.1. Prepare for and participate effectively in a range of conversations and collaborations with diverse partners, building on others' ideas and expressing their own clearly and persuasively.

CCRA.SL.2. Integrate and evaluate information presented in diverse media and formats, including visually, quantitatively, and orally.

CCRA.SL.3. Evaluate a speaker's point of view, reasoning, and use of evidence and rhetoric.

Speaking and Listening Standards 1, 2, and 3 address the ability to communicate successfully in a range of situations and with a range of partners, as when students communicate about a text they have closely read.

Presentation of Knowledge and Ideas

CCRA.SL.4. Present information, findings, and supporting evidence such that listeners can follow the line of reasoning and the organization, development, and style are appropriate to task, purpose, and audience.

CCRA.SL.5. Make strategic use of digital media and visual displays of data to express information and enhance understanding of presentations.

CCRA.SL.6. Adapt speech to a variety of contexts and communicative tasks, demonstrating command of formal English when indicated or appropriate.

The three standards under the Presentation of Knowledge and Ideas heading illustrate the importance of being able to organize and present information, part of which is understanding which register to use in different information-sharing contexts. Combined, these standards underscore the power of understanding language well enough to "interrogate" a text and glean the author's purpose or intent and of being able to use language precisely enough to convey a stance or argument. When readers interact with a text during a close reading, using language skills for in-depth analysis is exactly what they are doing. They need language proficiency both to comprehend the key ideas of the text and to scrutinize the author's use of language in order to identify additional ideas and details intended to promote an opinion or argument, share information, or entertain.

Supporting Effective Communication About Close Reading

The following instructional approaches and examples illustrate ways to support students' language use as they speak, listen, and write during and after a close reading. These routines demonstrate the interconnected relationship among language practices that can occur when students engage in reading and writing practices within a discipline. English language learners and their classmates have opportunities to "try on" both academic language and the language of the disciplines as they engage in these instructional routines.

Oral Communication Strategies

To quote Vygotsky (1978), "By giving our students practice in talking with others, we give them frames for thinking on their own" (p. 19).

Partner talk and small-group conversation. Participating effectively in conversation is a learned practice, and students must have opportunities to converse if they are to become more proficient in it. If the teacher doesn't take steps to nurture participation, the "whole-class discussions" of closely read texts can turn into a conversation between the teacher and just a few students.

A great first step toward avoiding that outcome is to invite partner talk or small-group conversation before students share their findings and ideas as a whole class. Speaking to only one or a few others builds speaking confidence in children who might initially feel uncomfortable speaking to the entire class. Text-dependent questions (*What was the main idea of the text? Where exactly did you find that information? What in the text made you think that? What language did the author use to contrast the two claims being made in the text?*) can provide the focus and the structures student pairs or small groups need for such conversation.

Conversational modeling and practice. You can teach "school talk," the language and behavior of the academic register, through a Fishbowl setting where you first engage with a few children and model how to participate in a small-group or partner discussion (see p. 134). Through regular participation in conversations about information gleaned from close text reading the use of awareness-boosting tools like the "Assessing My Speaking" guide shown in Figure 5.1, students learn the behaviors associated with academic communication, and it becomes a habit for them to use evidence to support their text interpretations.

Purposeful partner talk supported with sentence frames. *Turn to your partner and ____* is a very common phrase in close reading instruction, an alert to students that they are to discuss information they have encountered in the text or answer a question posed or perhaps brainstorm ideas in preparation for a follow-up writing activity. Generally speaking, today's students have become very good at turning to a peer and talking; whether they stick to the topic at hand rather than discuss their weekend, recess plans, or the latest video game is another question. Furthermore, although the intent of partner talk is to build responsive and collaborative language exchanges, the practice of partner talk can easily turn into students waiting to be heard rather than focusing on the partner's message. They can spend more time thinking about what they are going to say when their partner has (finally!) finished talking than truly listening to their partner's ideas.

Figure 5.1 | **A Student Self-Assessment for Academic Communication**   Download

Assessing My Speaking

When it was my turn to speak . . .

☐   I used a clear voice.

☐   I made eye contact with listeners.

☐   I stated information clearly and concisely.

☐   I shared text-based support for the ideas I shared.

☐   I invited questions.

☐   I listened to questions before responding.

☐   I invited and supported the participation of others.

☐   I asked others what they thought.

☐   I provided clarification or additional information when others asked me to.

☐   I brought up points others had made.

☐   I offered summary statements when appropriate.

Throughout the conversation . . .

☐   I paid attention to the speaker.

☐   I encouraged the speaker by nodding my head and looking pleasantly engaged.

☐   I asked appropriate questions.

☐   I challenged ideas in a respectful way.

☐   I asked the speaker to verify information using polite language.

☐   I allowed others a chance to participate.

☐   I gained insights from others.

☐   I shared confirming or alternate positions.

☐   I provided text-based support for my thinking.

☐   I encouraged the conversation through my responses and attention to the speaker(s).

Sentence frames, like those shown in Figure 5.2, can support focused and purposeful partner talk in which students extend, question, justify, or build on their partner's responses to a teacher's question. Amy Miles, who currently teaches 6th grade, regularly places laminated sets of sentence frames on her students' desks. She also used similar sentence frames with primary and intermediate grade students. When she wants them to focus on listening and conversing during partner talk about a text or topic that is being closely read, she refers them to the chart containing the kind of information shown in Figure 5.3—a combination of sentence frames and close reading annotations. This chart serves as a reference for students—both as they partner talk about the annotations they have made during a close reading and as they write about their ideas after a close reading.

Figure 5.2 | **Sentence Frames for Close Reading Conversations**

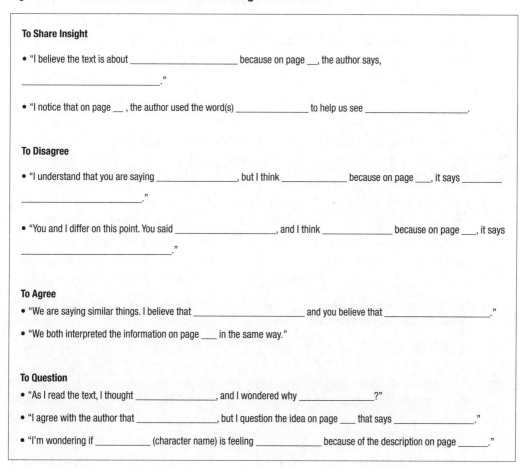

To Share Insight

• "I believe the text is about _____ because on page ___, the author says, _____."

• "I notice that on page ___ , the author used the word(s) _____ to help us see _____.

To Disagree

• "I understand that you are saying _____, but I think _____ because on page ____, it says _____ _____."

• "You and I differ on this point. You said _____, and I think _____ because on page ____, it says _____."

To Agree

• "We are saying similar things. I believe that _____ and you believe that _____."

• "We both interpreted the information on page ____ in the same way."

To Question

• "As I read the text, I thought _____, and I wondered why _____?"

• "I agree with the author that _____, but I question the idea on page ____ that says _____."

• "I'm wondering if _____ (character name) is feeling _____ because of the description on page _____."

Four Corners. This kinesthetic strategy, which gets students up and out of their seats to discuss their thoughts and ideas in different parts of the classroom, is a good way to teach argumentation while fostering engaged, purposeful, and productive conversation.

Here's an illustration. After leading the class in a close reading and large-group discussion of a segment of Robert Coles's *The Story of Ruby Bridges*, Juan Drake, a 3rd grade teacher, displayed the following statement on the document camera: *The real hero in the story was Ruby's teacher.* Mr. Drake invited the students to think about this statement based on information they had learned while reading the text. Then he asked them to move to one of the four corners of the room he had marked with signs reading *Strongly Agree, Agree, Disagree,* and *Strongly Disagree.* Once there, students discussed why they responded as they had to the statement and also listened to others' ideas. After several minutes of corner discussion, each small group "defended" its position to the rest of the class. Then, when all four groups had been heard from, students were free to move to a different corner if they had been persuaded by another group's case.

The conversation and argumentation that ensues from a Four Corners activity is a great way to build the academic language used in the texts students are closely reading and discussing.

Inside Outside Circles. This is another way to engage students physically and cognitively after a close reading, while also developing their academic language. Students form two large circles—an inner circle and an outer circle. Students in the inner circle face outward, those in the outer circle face inward, and students "partner" with the peer they are immediately facing. Once the stage is set, ask a text-dependent question. The inner-circle partner speaks first, and then the outer-circle partner. Once pairs of students have shared their ideas, the inner-circle students take a step to the right or left and share with a new partner. Here's an example of how it was used in a primary classroom to develop listening and speaking skills in concert with close reading instruction.

Angela Goss read aloud Lloyd Moss's *Zin! Zin! Zin! A Violin* to her 1st grade class several times. She posed text-dependent questions to send the children back to the poem, encouraging them to listen closely as she read and reread the numbered stanzas and engaged them in partner talk and table-talk discussions about the images the poem conveyed. Mrs. Goss wanted to be sure students understood the phrase "And so, good-bye to our new friends," so she asked everyone to stand up and form an inner and outer circle. The first question she

Figure 5.3 | **Visual Support for Purposeful Partner Talk**

Close Reading Annotations

Highlight = major points   **Circle** = confusing or unknown words/phrases
! = What surprises you   **?** = Questions you have

Make a Prediction

I think that _____ because _____.
I believe _____.
I predict _____.
I infer from this passage that _____,
which causes me to predict _____.
This information leads me to predict _____.

Ask a Question

I wonder _____.
How did _____?
What does the author mean when he/she
mentions _____.
Why does the author discuss _____?
What words did the author use to _____?
Why is it important to know _____?

Don't forget your margin notes!

Put It in Your Own Words

What _____ says is _____.
The author is basically saying _____.
The author mentions _____.
The gist of this passage/chapter/paragraph is
_____.
In short, this text is about _____.
In short, this _____ tells us _____.
From this passage, we learn _____.
The main idea of this passage is _____.

Clarify It

When the author states _____, he/she is
trying to _____.
The word _____ is used to _____.
When the author mentions _____, it tells
us _____.
The word _____ means _____.
To clarify, the author is saying that the difference
between _____ and _____.
is _____.

Courtesy of Amy Miles.

asked was, "Who are the new friends that are mentioned in the text, and how do you know?" (She anticipated that some pairs would not know how to answer.) Once the pairs had shared, Mrs. Goss asked the inner circle to take a step to the right so they would have another peer to talk and listen to. Then she repeated the question, knowing that allowing students to talk with multiple partners would likely generate multiple answers. As she engaged in formative assessment by listening in on student talk, Mrs. Goss heard evidence that Ariana was clarifying her thinking when the girl said, "Well, I said the new friends are the instruments, and you said the players of the music are the new friends. It's kind of the same." Mrs. Goss also heard Lila tell David, "As I read, I thought the people playing were the friends, and I wondered why we had to say 'a late goodnight' to them, like it says in the book." Based on what she was hearing during the partner exchanges, Mrs. Gross was able to ask more explicit questions that helped her 1st graders to deeper understanding of the content.

Gallery Walk. This structured activity is a good way to promote discussion of particular aspects of a topic following or prior to a close reading. It involves using a wall or desk space to display "works of art" and having students travel in groups to each station and discuss what they see. While at the stations, students might talk about questions that are posed, jot ideas on sticky notes, or watch a video clip and add notes to a Foldable®.

For example, after conversations with her 3rd graders indicated to Paola Escalante that they didn't have sufficient background knowledge to engage in a close reading of Kadir Nelson's *We Are the Ship: The Story of Negro League Baseball,* she posted a series of images of the Civil Rights movement. At each stop on this gallery tour, students paused for several minutes to discuss what they thought was happening in the image and used the posted sentence frames to structure their talk with peers. Listening in and gathering more formative assessment data, Ms. Escalante was able to refine the set of text-dependent questions she planned to use to further her students' understanding during the close reading to come.

Fishbowl. This is another effective way for students to learn about and practice effective collaborative conversation about close reading. During a Fishbowl, most of the class sits in a large circle. A few students (4–6) sit in a small, inner circle; they are the primary voice during the discussion. As the inner-circle students speak, those in the outer circle listen to the conversation, record main points, and write down questions of their own. You might include an empty chair in the inner circle so students can voluntarily come to the Fishbowl, offer an idea, and quickly return to the outer circle, freeing up the inner-circle chair for another student.

Consider a Fishbowl conducted by Kate Browning immediately after her 2nd graders closely read Chapter 4 of *Charlotte's Web*. Ms. Browning knew that several students had a firm grasp of how author E. B. White used foreshadowing to create mood, and she asked them to gather in the inner circle to talk about the evidence that supported foreshadowing in the text. To push them a little further, she asked guiding questions that focused them on comparing the foreshadowing in Chapter 4 of *Charlotte's Web* with the foreshadowing used in Christopher Paul Curtis's (1999) *Bud, Not Buddy*, a text students had read earlier in the year: *What language did these authors use that gave you clues about what to expect of the characters in either story? Did they use similar approaches?* Using these questions as the stepping off point, the students went on to ask questions of one another, clarify misconceptions, and support ideas with detailed evidence. Here are the sentence frames Ms. Browning posted to scaffold the discussion including a look at how her students filled in the blanks:

> I think Curtis chose the words <u>blanket, extra clothes, picture of mother, and flyers</u> to give us some insights about Bud's mission. He also gave other clues, like <u>Bud's missing the train,</u> that helped me to understand his mission. Do you think the rocks gave other clues about Bud's mission?

> When Charlotte says "<u>After all, what's a life, anyway? We're born, we live a little while, we die,</u>" on page 154, she is explaining to Wilbur that all things must die. I think the author used this conversation to suggest the struggles ahead for Wilbur. How did this conversation also give us clues about what would happen to Charlotte?

The resulting give-and-take was a model of how to engage in a conversation about a text or a feature of a text.

To ensure that a Fishbowl will provide a good model for other students, it's a good idea to practice ahead of time with the members of the inner circle. You can also invite other members of the class to ask questions of the "fish." This encourages everyone to share documented ideas, using academic language to do so.

Written Communication Strategies

Students also need to become well-versed in the various ways in which they can use writing to document their thinking as they respond to a closely read text. Oftentimes they struggle with incorporating appropriate evidence in a logical, academic-sounding manner. The following instructional approaches and examples illustrate ways to support students' written responses to closely read texts.

Generative Sentences. The Generative Sentences strategy can be used to help focus students on extracting and documenting evidence from a text to support their comprehension and thinking. Teachers can ask students to work with partners to *generate,* or create, sentences that focus on particular key words or on finding evidence from the text. For example, a teacher might ask students who are reading an informational text to work with a partner to write a sentence that includes a specific key word, like *retina* when reading about the structure of eyes, or *gibbous* when reading about lunar phases. When students seek out evidence from the text on an area of key word focus, they are being directed to center their thinking on main ideas. In this way, student-created sentences like *The retina is located at the back of the eye and is sensitive to light,* and *The gibbous moon appears a little less fully lit than a full moon* reveal student understanding.

To incorporate academic language and to take student thinking to a deeper level, a teacher might next ask partners to write a sentence in which they incorporate particular academic language. The academic language can be strategically chosen to guide student attention to a particular part of the text. For instance, a teacher who wants her students to better understand the function of the retina might ask her student partners to generate a sentence that uses this academic language *According to the text, the function of the retina* _____ or *Based on my understanding of the text, the role of the retina* _____. A sentence built using one of these frames (e.g., *According to the text, the function of the retina is to translate light into nerve signals*) can show evidence that students have gone back to the text to indentify key ideas.

GIST. Another way to get students to record both their thinking and the ideas generated from conversations they participate in between consecutive close reads is to have them work with partners or small teams using the GIST strategy (Cunningham, 1982). With this strategy, students focus on the *who, what, where, when, why,* or *how* (5Ws and 1H) of a piece of text. They write a 20-word *GIST*—a summary or explanation that addresses one or more of the 5Ws or the H. A teacher might first have students create their GISTs individually and then have them collaborate to synthesize their ideas into one joint GIST. For example, when reading a text about Martin Luther King Jr. and the 1963 March on Washington, Kiara, a 3rd grade student, might write a GIST about the H (how) this way: *Martin Luther King Jr. and others marched to help everyone get their rights. They heard Martin Luther King speak.* Her classmate Ethan might write: *Martin walked with people in Washington. He made an important speech about his dreams.* Where Kiara and Ethan combine their ideas, they might write this together: *Martin Luther King Jr. marched with people for equal rights. In a speech in Washington, D.C., he talked about his dreams for America.*

What's particularly valuable about the GIST strategy is that in order for students to pare down their ideas to only 20 words, they must discuss what is most important—what is essential—to answering their W or H question. It is oftentimes through peer conversations that students come to an understanding of central ideas. Clearly, this strategy holds the potential to link peer conversations to writing.

Writing as a Close Reading Connection

Like speaking, writing is both an expressive language process and a means of communication—a way to tell stories and to share information, positions, experiences, insights, and ideas. The purpose of sharing written discourse with an intended, but often unknown, audience provides the frame for the text. Instead of writing for only "the teacher" or for "no one in particular," students are asked to write to an audience. For example, they may write to a community board, to readers of a newspaper, to a member of Congress, or even to members of a nonprofit organization. All writing is produced with a purpose in mind, and the process of writing for an intended audience can clarify that purpose for the author. This authorial intent provides a frame for the reader's understanding.

The Common Core's writing standards map the skill development a student needs to graduate high school capable of communicating across disciplines with varied audiences for myriad purposes. The 10 anchor standards address writing to inform, explain, convey experiences both real and imagined, and argue a position —although in the elementary grades, students work not on argumentation but persuasion, or writing to share a supported opinion, which is a groundwork for presenting a well-documented stance and arguing its merits.

How is writing a dimension of a close reading experience? The most succinct response to this question is that each time students return to the text to look for evidence of an author's message or intent, they are doing so through an interplay with the language choices that author has made. Identifying these choices supports critical analysis not just of the message but also of how language has been employed to convey that message. Acquiring such insights furthers students' growth as writers as they "develop the capacity to build knowledge on a subject through research projects and to respond analytically to literary and informational sources" (NGA Center & CCSSO, 2010a, p. 18). Additionally, students develop the ability to evaluate, critique, and communicate about a text as they share their comprehension.

The Common Core's Writing Standards

The 10 anchor standards for writing are grouped under four headings: Text Types and Purposes, Production and Distribution of Writing, Research to Build and Present Knowledge, and Range of Writing. Let's explore the standards under each heading and their relationship with close text reading, and then look at instructional examples that promote writing as it relates to communicating about a text.

Text Types and Purposes

CCRA.W.1. Write arguments to support claims in an analysis of substantive topics or texts using valid reasoning and relevant and sufficient evidence.

CCRA.W.2. Write informative/explanatory texts to examine and convey complex ideas and information clearly and accurately through the effective selection, organization, and analysis of content.

CCRA.W.3. Write narratives to develop real or imagined experiences or events using effective technique, well-chosen details and well-structured event sequences.

Notice that in addition to identifying the three types of written texts students should be able to produce, each standard under this heading clearly specifies why there is value in being able to share ideas and information through multiple formats. Arguments, for example, are written to support a claim being made; informative/ explanatory texts are written to convey complex ideas and information across many topics; and narratives are crafted in ways that share real and imagined events or experiences.

Although the standards identify skill development across all three types of writing from as early as kindergarten, *argumentative writing* appears as *opinion writing* throughout the elementary years. For example, at the kindergarten level, Writing Standard 1 reads as follow:

W.K.1. Use a combination of drawing, dictating, and writing to compose opinion pieces in which they tell a reader the topic or the name of the book they are writing about and state an opinion or preference about the topic or book (e.g., *My favorite book is . . .*).

By 3rd grade, Writing Standard 1 is readying students to write arguments that take a stance, support it, and use linking words to connect or bridge the stance (claim) and facts.

> **W.3.1.** Write opinion pieces on topics or texts, supporting a point of view with reasons.
>
> a. Introduce the topic or text they are writing about, state an opinion, and create an organizational structure that lists reasons.
>
> b. Provide reasons that support the opinion.
>
> c. Use linking words and phrases (e.g., *because, therefore, since, for example*) to connect opinion and reasons.
>
> d. Provide a concluding statement or section.

Then, in 5th grade, Writing Standard 1 asks students to provide logically ordered reasons. It's a skill that they will use extensively in the later grades, when they are called on to write arguments.

> **W.5.1.** Write opinion pieces on topics or texts, supporting a point of view with reasons and information.
>
> a. Introduce a topic or text clearly, state an opinion, and create an organizational structure in which ideas are logically grouped to support the writer's purpose.
>
> b. Provide logically ordered reasons that are supported by facts and details.
>
> c. Link opinion and reasons using words, phrases, and clauses (e.g., *consequently, specifically*).
>
> d. Provide a concluding statement or section related to the opinion presented.

Finally, in 6th grade, the term *opinion* changes to *argument*:

> **W.6.1.** Write arguments to support claims with clear reasons and relevant evidence.
>
> a. Introduce claim(s) and organize the reasons and evidence clearly.
>
> b. Support claim(s) with clear reasons and relevant evidence, using credible sources and demonstrating an understanding of the topic or text.
>
> c. Use words, phrases, and clauses to clarify the relationships among claim(s) and reasons.

   d. Establish and maintain a formal style.

   e. Provide a concluding statement or section that follows from the argument
      presented.

Figure 5.4 highlights the subtle differences between *writing opinion pieces* (the persuasive writing students focus on in elementary school) and *crafting arguments* (the argumentative writing they will tackle in middle school). Notice how the skills associated with the former kind of writing are applied in the latter.

Although the emphasis in grades K–5 is on developing students' capacity to clearly and logically state an opinion that is rooted in evidence, it is critical for an elementary teacher to understand the trajectory students follow as they move toward argumentative writing in grades 6–12. An opinion statement notes a viewpoint and provides evidence from the text to clarify the statement. An effective written argument includes a *claim,* which is a conclusion that the writer makes based on *evidence,* which are the facts that he or she has identified. The *warrant* is the logical bridge connecting the claim and the evidence. *Counterclaims* offer an alternative position that the student or writer should discredit with additional evidence. In Figure 5.5, we share a progression of sentence frames that can help students as they learn to identify and write opinion statements that could ultimately move them toward an argumentative essay.

Figure 5.4 | **A Comparison of Persuasive Writing and Argumentative Writing**

Persuasive Writing	Argumentative Writing
Purpose: To convince reader of a point of view.	**Purpose:** To convince reader that the stance taken is a supported position worthy of consideration.
Author's Position: Shares one emotional or impassioned position with the intent of convincing reader to agree.	**Author's Position:** Acknowledges that there may be multiple perspectives on a topic but uses data to show that there is only one stance or conviction that is worthwhile to believe.
Audience: An identified audience the author is attempting to persuade.	**Audience:** No specific audience needs to be identified. The author is attempting to share a viable position on a topic.
Composing Technique: The author combines some fact with emotion in an attempt to convince.	**Composing Technique:** The author combines well-documented facts, evidence, connections or warrants, counterclaims, and rebuttals to present a position of substance.
Writing Process: The author identifies a position within a topic and shares an emotionally driven justification to gain the reader's agreement.	**Writing Process:** The author researches a topic thoroughly; makes a claim/takes a stance; supports the claim with evidence; examines a counterclaim; creates the bridging link, or warrant, between the claim and the evidence and shares a rebuttal to refute the counterclaim in support of the original stance; and summarizes the claim.

Figure 5.5 | **Step-by-Step Sentence Frames for Argumentative Writing**

Step 1: Take a stance/*make a claim.*

• Because of evidence found on page ___ suggesting that _____, I believe that _____. Therefore my claim, or stance, is _____.

Step 2: Provide *evidence* to support your claim.

• I believe my position is worthwhile because _____. Other evidence to support my analysis is that _____. This information promotes my belief that _____.

Step 3: Acknowledge a *counterclaim.*

• While _____ believes _____, I remain convinced that _____, because _____.

• An alternate position might be _____, but I maintain that _____, because _____.

Step 4: Provide a *warrant* (a commonsense bridge between the claim and the evidence).

• I believe _____ (claim), because _____ (evidence) and _____ (commonsense warrant).

• Based on my observation that _____ (evidence) and the facts that suggest _____ (evidence), I believe _____ (claim). Furthermore, _____ (commonsense warrant) suggests that _____ (claim).

• However, _____ (counterclaim), but the facts—namely, _____ (evidence)—support my original stance that _____ (claim).

Step 5: *Summarize* your claim.

• To conclude, I maintain that _____. This is a reasonable stance because evidence that _____ and _____ overwhelmingly support the conclusion that _____.

For further clarification on the difference between presenting a written opinion and making a written argument, consider the following student response, generated after a close reading of a text on the global effects of fishing on biodiversity:

Fishing too much can hurt the ocean environment. In paragraph two of our article, it says that we need different kinds of fish to have a healthy ocean. Big fish eat little fish, and if some of the little fish are gone, the big ones won't have food. If people catch the big fish, there will be too many little fish. This could affect the food web in the ocean. I think that people need to stop fishing so much. We need to keep the coral reefs and other parts of the ocean full of many different kinds of fish.

This is persuasive writing, generated by a 5th grader; it's a statement of opinion that contains some text-based facts. Now, consider how this text might look if the writer were a 6th grader tasked with writing an argument. See if you can spot the claim, the presentation of the counterclaim, the documentation, and the writer's final stance:

> Overfishing can hurt the marine environment. We need a variety of fish in the ocean to have biodiversity. If we don't, that's a problem. A report by the United Nations says that commercial fish populations of cod, hake, and flounder are lower now, by 95 percent, in the North Atlantic Ocean. Some people think that we shouldn't worry about overfishing because people need to fish for food. Two hundred million people fish. Lots of them are in poor countries. Some people think that if we stop them from fishing by making rules about how much you can catch, they won't have food. Even though this might be true, a bigger problem is overfishing. If we overfish, soon we won't have any fish. We need biodiversity—lots of different kinds of fish in the ocean to have a healthy environment.

While our focus in this book is on persuasive and opinion writing, it is helpful to be familiar with the progression that students will take from opinion writing to argumentative writing. In order to effectively share an opinion or make an argument, either in writing or orally, students need more than just a grasp of how persuasion and argumentation are constructed. They also need facility with language, particularly a grasp of which register to use, which is addressed in Speaking and Listening Standard 4 (see CCRA.SL.4, p. 128). Although teachers may set out to design learning experiences to address one particular standard, there is high probability that other standards will be involved at the same time. As the instructional context changes from a partner chat during a close reading to a topical debate and then to a written response, ELA standards can be integrated to support language skill development across grades and situations.

Production and Distribution of Writing

CCRA.W.4. Produce clear and coherent writing in which the development, organization, and style are appropriate to task, purpose, and audience.

CCRA.W.5. Develop and strengthen writing as needed by planning, revising, editing, rewriting, or trying a new approach.

CCRA.W.6. Use technology, including the Internet, to produce and publish writing and to interact and collaborate with others.

The standards under this heading address the skills involved in planning, writing, and then publishing text. As the heading indicates, the very carefully developed process of writing a text is influenced by its purpose and intended audience. We find it interesting that collaboration via the Internet is identified as a dimension of both the production of text and its publication.

Research to Build and Present Knowledge

CCRA.W.7. Conduct short as well as more sustained research projects based on focused questions, demonstrating understanding of the subject under investigation.

CCRA.W.8. Gather relevant information from multiple print and digital sources, assess the credibility and accuracy of each source, and integrate the information while avoiding plagiarism.

CCRA.W.9. Draw evidence from literary or informational texts to support analysis, reflection, and research.

Writing Standards 7, 8, and 9 focus on the skills associated with researching, analyzing, validating, and reflecting on topically related sources of information. Notice how these standards highlight the writing of well-researched and well-documented texts of varying lengths. Investigating multiple sources, both informational and literary, as part of the writing process calls for the kind of in-depth analysis students engage in during a close reading.

Range of Writing

CCRA.W.10. Write routinely over extended time frames (time for research, reflection, and revision) and shorter time frames (a single sitting or a day or two) for a range of tasks, purposes, and audiences.

Although there is only one standard under the Range of Writing heading, it is a comprehensive one, encouraging students' regular engagement in writing tasks that promote the ability to write many text types of alternate lengths with multiple purposes and for an array of audiences. One intention implicit in this standard is that writing be done routinely and for longer spans of time so that it becomes an expected component of instruction within every discipline.

Supporting Understanding of Written Language Use

Students learn about written language by observing how authors use it to inform, entertain, and persuade. It's important to build into close reading sessions a variety of listening, speaking, and writing activities that draw students' attention to the craft of writing. Here are some tools for doing so.

Writer's Reference Notebooks. Before beginning a close reading, invite students to create a personal Writer's Reference Notebook where they can keep track of how authors use language to convey information, to entertain, to convince and persuade, and so on. You can have students use labeled dividers to create separate sections focusing on different aspects of the authors' language use: "Word Choices," "Unique Features of the Text," "Imagery," and so on.

In close reading, the multiple returns to a text that help students acquire a deeper understanding of its information also give them the opportunity to explore author's use of language. To encourage such rereading, ask students to go back to the text for a specific, language-focused purpose, such as to identify which words make them "see" or "hear" the author's voice. They can record their findings in a "Word Choice" section of their Writer's Reference Notebook along with other words, phrases, and sentences that they feel were artfully used.

For example, in the science text *Volcanoes*, a Common Core text exemplar for grades 4–5, author Seymour Simon describes the various forms that volcanoes can take while exploring particular volcanoes around the world. He does so using words such as *molten, eruption,* and *fiery rivers.* During one rereading, in Matt Peters's 4th grade classroom, students were asked to record and comment on language that Simon used that made the text more accessible, interesting, and informative for them. To clarify for students, Mr. Peters shared that the language used by Simon made him visualize red, hot lava spilling out of a volcano to form something that is like a pool of water but is really hot, melted rock material. During another close reading, Mr. Peters asked students to return to the text to spot techniques the author used to share ideas. In *Volcanoes,* students noticed how the author used contrastive analysis (a common feature of science writing) to share information about energy released from the eruption of Mount St. Helens and to describe the cracks in the Earth's crust. Simon compares the released energy to 10 million tons of dynamite, and he connects the Earth's broken crust to a giant cracked eggshell. The technique was included in the Writer's Reference Notebook in a section for "Unique Text Features" along with indication of where in the text it was found.

Students should be encouraged to use the evidence they gather in these notebooks to support their discussions of the text and to inform their techniques as a writer.

Socratic Circles. Socrates was a famous champion of using artful discussion to logically examine the validity of an idea. Instruction that supports such dialogue is referred to as a Socratic Circle (Copeland, 2005).

When students in Carol Marlow's 5th grade class read about nuclear energy as a viable alternative form of energy, they examined concerns about nuclear reactor shutdowns and equipment failures alongside the perspective that nuclear energy is cheaper and cleaner than some other forms of energy. The two texts selected by Miss Marlow were "How Nuclear Power Works," an article by Marshall Brain and Robert Lamb published on Howstuffworks.com, and "Nuclear Power & the Environment," an article posted on the website of the U.S. Energy Information Administration. Based on their close reading of these two texts, students posed and discussed questions (e.g., *Could the use of nuclear energy slow down global warming? What happened to people near Chernobyl or Fukushima when those reactors had meltdowns?*). Miss Marlow then divided then into an inner and outer circles. Those in the inner circle posed and discussed additional questions about the text. Miss Marlow allowed students to create open-ended questions that might have more than one answer. Her goal was to prompt students to think about the text closely so that they could establish opinions rooted in evidence. Those in the outer circle listened, took notes, jotted down questions, and later shared the additional insights about the text they'd acquired from observing the discussion.

Following the Socratic Circle discussion, Miss Marlow asked students to work with partners to develop a critique of the articles in which they established their own ideas and understandings based on an in-depth discussion of the risks of nuclear reactor use, the most recent technological advancements in nuclear energy, and the benefits of nuclear energy use. Miss Marlow provided these language frame options and then asked partners to incorporate at least two of these into their writing:

Despite the fact that _____, we believe _____.

Considering the evidence, _____.

We do not agree that _____ because _____.

The data shows that _____.

Through this activity, Miss Marlow's students gained experience in all of the following: (1) the consideration of multiple perspectives of an issue through the reading of two texts, (2) discussion in an in-depth, inquiry-based manner, and (3) writing experience based on the close reading of two texts and informed by analytical conversations.

Depth of Knowledge–Based Questioning. Depth of Knowledge (DOK) is a process for analyzing the complexity of standards and assessments that was created by Norman Webb (see Webb, et al., 2005) and is widely used by educators to help students to access content in more profound ways. The DOK levels are Recall (Level 1), Skill or Concept (Level 2), Strategic Thinking (Level 3), and Extended Thinking (Level 4). Strategically developed text-dependent questions can help drive the reader to increasingly higher DOK levels:

- Level 1 questions might ask the student to *identify the main idea* or *list key ideas.* Answers to these types of questions help manifest a foundational understanding of the text.
- Level 2 questions might require that the student *summarize the events* or *interpret data from a chart or graph.* Questions from this level guide students to home in on specific areas of a text so that they can note ways in which language is used to show how events progressed, show how evidence or ideas are connected to form patterns, or show particular events in a certain situation.
- Level 3 questions might move the reader to *form conclusions based on multiple forms of data presented* or to *cite evidence to help formulate an understanding of a key term like "civil disobedience"* or even to *identify how the author constructed his/her argument or perspective using different pieces of evidence.* These questions drive students to think more deeply as they identify potential research questions or investigations or as they create models to help understand problem or situation.
- Level 4 questions ask readers to go even further, into the realm of extended thinking.

Here is what DOK-based questioning looks like in the classroom. When Naima James engaged her 3rd grade students in a close reading of the Common Core text exemplar *Discovering Mars: The Amazing Story of the Red Planet* by Melvin Berger, she moved them from Level 1 text-dependent recall questions to Level 3 text-dependent strategic thinking questions over the course of three readings. Once Ms. James was satisfied that her students had a significant understanding of the content, she moved them toward DOK Level 4 by requiring them to work with partners to develop a plan to study an aspect of Mars that they had read about in the text.

Ms. James modeled the process using a different planet as an example—planet Earth. She told her students that she had recently read an article discussing how rivers flow across land. Because of this, she wanted to study how the Mississippi River flowed across the United States. She developed a series of questions related to her ideas: *How does the Mississippi River bend? What direction does it flow? Why does it flow?* These questions, she explained, would guide her further reading and research. Then Ms. James got her students started on the first step of this extended thinking task by having them brainstorm research questions related to their reading of the Mars text. Marcus and Michelle wanted to investigate mountains on Mars. Sheila and Elle were determined to study the possibility of life on Mars. Ultimately, mini research studies grew out of these questions, and student-made posters illustrating their creative plans for study were displayed around the classroom. DOK Level 4 questions are great springboards to writing that occurs post-reading.

Here are a few examples of other tasks at the Level 4 DOK that students might engage in after a close reading:

- Generate additional questions that connect the content to real-world, relevant issues. Then use additional resources to seek answers to the questions and determine a user group that could benefit from the information. Share the information in various formats—a podcast, a skit, a poster, a graphic cartoon, and so on.
- Analyze a problem mentioned in the text and create a solution (by building a product, writing a proposal, etc.).
- Critique a current solution to a real-world situation, identify areas of weakness and areas of strength, and design a revised plan.
- Apply concepts learned to create and design a solution/product/service to address a real-world problem or issue.

Karen Hess created a chart correlating Bloom's taxonomy with Webb's Cognitive Matrix—otherwise known as the Degrees of Knowledge. It's a good resource for supporting students' deep inquiry into text, and is available online at http://static.pdesas.org/content/documents/M1-Slide_22_DOK_Hess_Cognitive_Rigor.pdf.

Power Writing. Close reading demands that students return to a text numerous times to conduct deeper and deeper analysis. This requires focus, stamina, and a well-developed understanding of language use. To build this kind of stamina (and promote language fluency), Fearn and Farnan (2001) advocate power writing, a daily "structured free-write where the objective is quantity alone" (p. 501). In power writing, either the teacher or a student offers a topic in the form of a word (e.g., *magnets, football, stars*) or phrase (e.g., *sugar is good and bad, new shoes, at the zoo*). Students have one minute to write as much as they can, as well as they can. When time is up, each student counts the number of words he or she has written and records it in the page margin. Then the cycle repeats twice: two more one-minute writing sessions on different topics, with the documentation of the number of words written. At the conclusion of the third cycle, students return to each writing sample to circle and correct any words they believe they misspelled; the number of errors made and caught provides assessment information on the students' self-monitoring ability. Students convert the word counts into a visual documentation of their developing fluency, charting the longest response of the day over a series of days and eventually pasting a graph into their notebooks as a private record of their progress.

Writing RAFTs. The RAFT writing strategy (Santa & Havens, 1995) is an effective tool for helping students grasp the point of view of a character in text they are reading closely, for calling their attention to how perspective functions in literature, and for focusing them on how both audience and format can shape the message of a written text.

When writing a RAFT, students must consider the following:

Role of the Writer: What perspective/voice are you assuming? (a pilgrim, a citizen, a piece of chocolate)
Audience: To whom are you writing? (a turkey, a member of Congress, the digestive system)
Format: What form will the message take? (a speech, a letter, a poem)
Topic: What is the topic of the message? (celebrations, taxes, eating habits)

For example, after participating in close thinking as their teacher read aloud *Are You My Mother?* by P. D. Eastman, kindergarten students could create a RAFT response in which *R* = Mother, *A* = baby, *F* = storyboard drawing, and *T* = where you can find me.

In other words, assuming the character of the mother, students draw in different boxes of the storyboard all the places where the baby bird could have found her throughout the story. Similarly, after a close reading of Carl Sandburg's "Fog," 4th grade students focusing on the author's poetic style and language use might write a RAFT from the perspective of the Sandburg himself in which R = Carl Sandburg, A = 4th grade reader, F = poem, and T = the wind.

Having students write from the perspective of another character, author, or person they have just explored in a close reading is a way to assess their writing proficiencies and also learn a great deal about their comprehension of the text.

Writing Scavenger Hunt. Writers search their minds and notes for the right detail, the perfect setting, and the ideal character description. Authors choose their words very carefully, and one way for students to examine such powerful language is to participate in a writing scavenger hunt. During this engaging task, students return to closely read text to find a "list of items." For example, Greg Botham, a 2nd grade teacher, created a "list of items" for his students to find while closely reading Chapter 4 of *The Lighthouse Family: The Storm* by Cynthia Rylant (2003). As you can see in Figure 5.6, Mr. Botham constructed these items to guide inquiry into how the author uses language to shape the reader's impression of characters.

Cindy Pham engaged her 5th grade students in a writing scavenger hunt of a different kind. After her students did a close reading from a chapter in the Common Core text exemplar *Flight to Freedom: The Story of the Underground Railroad* by Henrietta Buckmaster, Miss Pham directed them to an online collection of historical photographs and provided them with the second item list in Figure 5.6., which guided them through these nonprint texts and led into a writing activity and a rich discussion.

Students will develop and learn to use academic language when they are invited and taught to do so. As Miller & Calfee (2004) note,

> [An] individual may experience great internal delight after struggling with a message and finally "getting it." But how can external observers (teachers and researchers) tap into this experience, assuming a good reason for such an attempt? The most direct and comprehensive approach is to ask the individual to present the results of the activity, by retelling, summarizing, applying, critiquing, extending, transforming, and so on—in brief, by composing some sort of response. (p. 229)

Figure 5.6 | **Two Lists for Writing Scavenger Hunts**

Mrs. Botham's List of Items for Chapter 4 of Rylant's *The Lighthouse Family: The Storm*

☐ Find the word describes how Pandora got out of bed? Write it here: _____

☐ Find the description of what Seabold and Pandora did all morning. What did they do? _____

_____

☐ Find what Seabold and Pandora were doing as they "painted the world pink and red" Describe it here: _____

_____

☐ Find and finish this sentence: *She saved them, thought Seabold. He watched his friend in* _____ .

☐ Find the explanation of why Pandora felt empty in her heart and write the page number here: _____ . Why did she feel this

way? _____

☐ **Writing Task:** This chapter is called "Companions." How have the characters changed since the beginning of the book? Use your answers above to help you respond.

_____

_____

_____

Miss Pham's List of Items Related to Buckmaster's *Flight to Freedom: The Story of the Underground Railroad*

(Text: Underground Railroad photographs at www.history.com/topics/black-history/underground-railroad/photos)

☐ Find the photo that is most disturbing to you. Explain why:

_____

_____

☐ Find the photo that best helps you understand the geography of the Underground Railroad. Explain why: _____

_____

☐ Find the photo that best helps you visualize how the slaves felt. Which words in the captions help with this? _____

_____

☐ Find the slave trade monument photos. What do they tell you about what was happening at this time? _____

_____

_____

_____

≕◈≔

The Common Core State Standards give us hope that the interrelated processes of language, writing, and reading will be taught as such. Close reading, the discussion it involves, and the follow-up activities it can lead to provide an excellent context for developing these proficiencies, which will, in turn, enhance students' ability to learn from texts. In Chapter 6, we'll examine how teachers, during a close reading, can assess students for the purpose of making informed and helpful "next step" decisions about instruction.

CHAPTER 6

ASSESSING TO SUPPORT MEANING MAKING DURING CLOSE READING

How do we assess students' performance during close reading? To begin to answer this question, pause and think about how you assess the performance of your students on any instructional task. Then think about *why* you assess their performance.

Wise teachers assess student performance and progress not just to assign grades but also to identify strengths and needs as related to the accomplishment of an identified learning purpose or objective. They know that assessment isn't a single event that takes place at the end of a lesson or unit; it's a process of collecting data to inform decisions about the best next step to support student learning, given students' growing strengths and changing needs (Lapp, Fisher, Flood, Cabello, 2001).

This process—the recursive cycle of using evidence of student understanding to adjust instructional practice—is what Popham (2008), Frey and Fisher (2011), and others describe as *formative assessment.* It has become increasingly familiar in today's classrooms, and the explanation for this is simple: formative assessment helps to improve student learning because it provides teachers with insights regarding their students' learning progress toward well-defined goals. Students who are in the classrooms of teachers who employ formative assessment practices outperform students in other classes. After conducting a comprehensive review of the research related to formative assessment practices, Black and Wiliam (1998) concluded that "Innovations that include strengthening the practice of formative assessment produce significant and often substantial learning gains" (p. 140). Hattie and Timperley (2007) found a 29 percent gain in achievement for students in classrooms with teachers who employed a formative assessment cycle; this was almost double the gains made by students in classrooms where teachers employed other, more traditional forms of assessment.

The gathering of performance-based insights through formative assessment is a very critical feature of close reading instruction, as these insights provide an ongoing means of supporting a student's comprehension growth. Here's how it plays out. Once a teacher has determined the purpose for closely reading a selected passage during the instructional planning stage and has identified the related performance task(s), he or she can assess the understanding students are sharing through their annotations, partner and whole-class collaborations, and written responses. Student responses also offer insights about their developing self-awareness as close readers. Collecting these mental and written notes while listening in, observing, and discussing a text with students provides the data a teacher needs to inform subsequent instructional decisions.

Formative assessment during instruction is an ongoing process—and this is no less the case when it's done in conjunction with close reading. The growth that occurs through this process of formatively assessing student performance as related to identified standards and adjusting instruction to address students' identified strengths and needs prepares them for the PARCC and Smarter Balanced summative assessments that are also aligned with the Common Core standards (see Chapter 1).

In this chapter, we examine the cycle of formative assessment as a pathway to gather insights about the comprehension that is occurring for students as they engage in a close analysis of texts across the disciplines. Our purpose is to emphasize how formative assessment supports teachers as they observe a student's performance, and then working from these observed behaviors, provide instructional scaffolds to further students' growth as readers who understand how to deeply analyze texts. We also illustrate how the scaffolded instruction that occurs as a result of formative assessment can be aligned with the Common Core standards that are aligned with the PARCC and Smarter Balanced summative assessments.

An Overview of the Formative Assessment Cycle

Formative assessment is an ongoing process that asks teachers to *identify* standards, *plan* related instruction, *teach*, *asses* student performance, *analyze* collected information to identify patterns of student need, and *plan* forward steps or revisions to instruction that will address the perceived needs. The goal is to use continually collected performance data to plan additional instruction and interventions to help all students achieve the identified standards.

For a classroom teacher, the cycle of formative assessment begins with identifying the lesson purpose, making note of the standards that will serve as the foundation for the lesson, and planning instruction in logical, purposeful segments that will advance students, step by step, toward the achievement of those standards. Although an initial, big-picture pre-assessment may help a teacher identify teaching points that, when addressed, will enable students to achieve identified standards, this is just the beginning of a formative assessment cycle. At predetermined points within the lesson, the teacher takes a measure of student progress, quickly analyzes data gathered, and alters instruction and instructional tasks as needed to continue moving all students toward the learning goal.

Guided instruction occurring during the *we do it* phase of the Gradual Release of Responsibility instructional framework (Grant, Lapp, Fisher, Johnson, & Frey, 2012; Pearson & Gallagher, 1983), in which a teacher works closely with students, provides excellent opportunities for formatively assessing how well individual students are learning information that will help them reach each learning target. Teachers can also gather formative assessment data by monitoring students' verbal responses to direct questions, partner-talk conversations, lab reports, collaborative participation, quizzes, exit and entry slips, response logs, graphic organizers, presentations, writing samples, self-assessments, and any other work samples that provide evidence regarding current learning.

In short, formative assessment provides the path to connect national and grade-level standards, learning targets, instruction, and continuous insights. It's a way to identify how well you are teaching and how well your students are learning. Well-planned formative assessment provides very precise information that will allow you to effectively scaffold instruction in order to address your students' different needs, build on their strengths, and provide better access to challenging curriculum.

Formative Assessment and Close Reading

The formative cycle of teaching and assessment starts with the teacher identifying the standards-related learning targets that contain well-articulated, identifiable measures of success. It continues with the teacher identifying "assessment points" —the places within the lesson where he or she will gather, formally or informally, data about the learning that is occurring and use that data to make an instructional adjustment.

As illustrated in Figure 6.1, the formative assessment cycle informs close reading instruction in much the same way. The identified lesson purpose is the goal for the close reading—and it generally includes CCRA.R.1 in addition to whatever disciplinary standards may be involved. The assessment points can be mapped to the various readings, teaching points, or features of the text, and the assessment tools include observation of students' annotations and independent reading behaviors, student comments in their partner talks/discussions, student responses to direct questioning, student self-assessments (like the one in Figure 5.1; see p. 130), students' written follow-up work, and students' behaviors during reading. The instructional adjustments are often revisions to the planned text-dependent questions, but they can also be new instructional modes/groupings or instructional sessions to backfill knowledge or vocabulary.

Figure 6.1 | **Formative Assessment Within Close Reading Instruction**

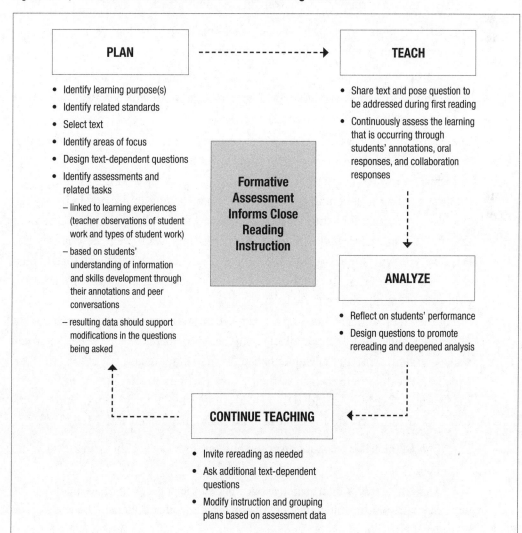

PLAN

- Identify learning purpose(s)
- Identify related standards
- Select text
- Identify areas of focus
- Design text-dependent questions
- Identify assessments and related tasks
  - linked to learning experiences (teacher observations of student work and types of student work)
  - based on students' understanding of information and skills development through their annotations and peer conversations
  - resulting data should support modifications in the questions being asked

Formative Assessment Informs Close Reading Instruction

TEACH

- Share text and pose question to be addressed during first reading
- Continuously assess the learning that is occurring through students' annotations, oral responses, and collaboration responses

ANALYZE

- Reflect on students' performance
- Design questions to promote rereading and deepened analysis

CONTINUE TEACHING

- Invite rereading as needed
- Ask additional text-dependent questions
- Modify instruction and grouping plans based on assessment data

The following scenario provides an example of how a 4th grade teacher, Maddie Lee, revised her science instruction as a result of information gleaned while listening to her students' conversation about a text they were closely reading—the Common Core informational text exemplar *Horses*, by Seymour Simon. Three standards guided this close reading session: the Common Core's Reading Anchor Standard 1, its 4th grade version in the Informational Text domain, and a 4th grade standard from the Life Cycles domain of the Next Generation Science Standards focused on structures and processes:

> **CCRA.R.1.** Read closely to determine what the text says explicitly and to make logical inferences from it; cite specific textual evidence when writing or speaking to support conclusions drawn from the text.

> **RI.4.2.** Quote accurately from a text when explaining what the text says explicitly and when drawing inferences from the text.

> **4-LS1-1.** Construct an argument that plants and animals have internal and external structures that function to support survival, growth, behavior, and reproduction.

The lesson purpose was for students to understand the structures of an animal (horses) and explain how these structures affect behavior.

Mrs. Lee always begins her close reading lessons by asking students to do the first reading independently, preparing them for possible struggle by saying, "I know that you will encounter new words and unfamiliar phrases. Remember that you should persist—keep going, keep reading. With each new reading of this text, you will gain more understanding. You will also have the chance to chat with your classmates. Through your conversations, you will work together to gain insights about the text."

For the first reading of *Horses*, Mrs. Lee had all students focus on text-dependent question about the text's overall meaning: *What information is Seymour Simon sharing in this text?* After all students had finished reading and annotating the text, Mrs. Lee directed them to turn to their elbow partners to share their responses to the first question. She reminded them to accurately quote lines from the text as evidence for their interpretations. She listened in as Chad talked with Molly:

> *Chad:* I think this is about horses and how fast they can go. They can *gait*—I think that means they go really fast—and they can gallop.

> *Molly:* And there's information about what they look like. Some have markings and some are different kinds of browns. It says that right here: *Brown*

horses range in color from dark brown bays and chestnuts to golden browns, such as palominos, and lighter browns, such as roans and duns. I didn't know there were so many kinds of brown. I don't even know what a *roan or dun* is.

Based on this interaction and various others she observed, Mrs. Lee concluded that her students understood that Simon was sharing information about various types of horses. Chad and Molly didn't have all the vocabulary words used in the text, but they were able to comprehend that the text was providing information about different horses. She focused in on Chad's unfamiliarity with the term *gait* and decided her next text-dependent question would require students to look at the details regarding different ways a horse can move. She made a note to develop a third question that focused on content language and classification—specifically on the various names for different types of horses. Using the information she gathered from listening to students talk, Mrs. Lee asked students to read the text a second time to note key details: "What are the different ways a horse can move, and how can you connect these to the speed of the horse? Be sure you continue to annotate the text."

Following the second close reading, Mrs. Lee again asked students to turn to their partners to share their responses to the text-dependent question. She heard Lila tell Mary that not only had she found all the ways the text said a horse can move, but she had also put those movements in order, from fastest to slowest: *gallop, canter, trot,* and *walk.* When Mrs. Lee reached Chad, she heard him say (again) that *gait* meant a fast movement. It was time for a direct intervention:

Mrs. Lee: Chad, would you reread the first sentence for me, please?

Chad: Uh-huh. *Horses move in four natural ways, called gaits or paces.*

Mrs. Lee: OK, so what is gait, according to that sentence? Go ahead and read it again.

Chad: Horses move in four natural ways, called gaits or paces. Oh, *gaits* means a way of moving.

Mrs. Lee (nodding): Is a gait always fast?

Chad: . . . If a gait is a way of moving, it could be fast, slow, or in between. Is that right?

Mrs. Lee: Yes, terrific thinking. You stuck with this text, and you read it so well. Good work!

It was now time to make some larger connections and address some lingering confusion in the process. Mrs. Lee glanced down at the clipboard holding an observation form set up with prepared text-dependent questions, notes about students' comments—including Molly's earlier expressed confusion about *roan* and *dun*, and notes about new questions to ask. (Figure 3.11, on p. 87, shows a template for this kind of observation form). After a moment spent reviewing her data, she turned to the rest of the class and said, "For the next close reading, I'd like you to focus on the technical terms used to describe the look of horses. The author, Seymour Simon, mentions several names for horses that are based on their coat color and markings. As you read, note these names and respond to this question: *How does the naming of horses based on coloring compare to other classification methods that we've studied in science?*"

Classification is a common organization method in science. This text-dependent question was strategically intended to help students connect the idea of classification in science to this particular informational text. After the third close reading, Mrs. Lee again listened in as Lila and Mary discussed classification of the horses by color:

> *Lila:* How can naming horses by color be like classifying animals and plants into different kingdoms? Is it like how we put different kinds of rocks into groups—igneous, sedimentary, and metamorphic? I'm not really sure about this.
>
> *Mary:* Look at all the names of horses here . . . *bays, chestnuts, palominos, roans, duns.* I didn't know there were so many names. I thought they were just all called horses!

Again, Mrs. Lee stepped in to provide clarification through questioning.

> *Mrs. Lee:* Why do we put some organisms into the kingdom of plants and some into the kingdom of animals? Why are some rocks metamorphic and others igneous?
>
> *Mary:* Because they have things in common with the group they are in. All igneous rocks are from lava or magma, and all metamorphic rocks are changed from heat or pressure. Is that right?
>
> *Mrs. Lee:* That *is* right. OK, now look at the text again. Do all piebalds have something in common—something other than being horses? Do all pintos have something in common?

Lila: ... Yes! All pintos are partly colored, and all piebalds have black and white patches. They have something in common when they have a name like *piebalds.* That's what classification is all about—having something in common. I've got it now.

Through her use of formative assessment during close reading and guided instruction, Mrs. Lee was able to address the specific learning needs of individual students. She was able to stem confusion and misconceptions, hone their evidence-finding skills, and move them toward a deeper level of understanding of the text and a key scientific concept.

When the learning targets are explicit, you can design both instruction and assessment measures to target the extent of the learning that occurs for each student. Insights about how well students are learning provide the information you need to alter instruction to accommodate student differences concerning standards-related learning targets.

Here's another example. In Laura Rosen's 4th grade class, students were closely reading diagrams of waves as part of a lesson addressing Next Generation Science Standard 4-PS4-1 ("Develop a model of waves to describe patterns in terms of amplitude and wavelength and that waves can cause objects to move") (NGSS Lead States, 2013). The students' textbook included clear drawings of transverse and longitudinal waves with all wave anatomy labeled, including crests, troughs, and the measures of amplitude and wavelength. She also set up learning stations with springs, ropes, ripple tanks, corks, eyedroppers, large pans, and access to water.

To begin this lesson, Ms. Rosen asked the whole class to closely read the wave diagrams to get an understanding of the information being shared. After they concluded and engaged in partner conversation, she focused a second reading of the diagrams by asking students this text-dependent question about a key detail of this text: *What features do the two types of waves seen in the diagrams—the transverse and the longitudinal waves—have in common?* Students again examined the diagrams and noted the captions, as is common practice in Ms. Rosen's class. (In the past, they had closely read diagrams of the human eye and of layers of rock.) After this round of reading and annotating, Ms. Rosen asked students to chat in pairs about the features they found on both diagrams. She listened in to determine the degree of their comprehension. By doing so, she initiated formative assessment.

Dave: Both transverse and longitudinal waves have a wavelength. See here? Below the pictures it says that *Wavelength is how long it is from crest to crest, or from trough to trough.* I wonder if it's the same length from crest to crest as it is from trough to trough. It looks like it is.

Ms. Rosen noted Dave's astute comment and moved on to a new set of partners, Claire and Elisa.

Elisa: I don't think these two waves are at all alike. I don't get what the little balls are in this picture. And why does this one have squiggly lines? What are waves anyway? This is so confusing!

Claire: The balls? See there? In the box on the right that says *Key,* it says that the balls are air molecules. I think this picture is showing how sound moves through the air.

At that point, Elisa, still looking puzzled, put her head on the desk. It was clear to Ms. Rosen that, as she had suspected, she would need to take a differentiated approach in order to help both struggling students like Elisa and students ready for extended challenge like Dave to continue to move their learning forward.

Ms. Rosen divided the class into small groups and sent them to various learning stations for hands-on activities. Station 1 had an investigation tool—a ripple tank with a wave generator. At this station, students were directed to look at how a cork moves as waves are created. They recorded observational data in their science notebooks. At Station 2, students created waves of differing frequencies using a computer simulation. Station 3 had students working together to solve period and frequency problems. And at Station 4, the teacher station, Ms. Rosen met with Elisa and four students who were English language learners to look at how models like those in the textbook diagrams represent real-world science phenomena. To foster better understanding, Ms. Rosen asked the group to view animations of transverse and longitudinal waves and thought aloud as she viewed the animations. Then she asked the students in this small group to think aloud with partners to describe what was similar and what was different. She ended by having this group reread the original diagrams to be sure that they now had the skills for successful comprehension.

As evidenced in this scenario, Ms. Rosen and the entire 4th grade class were engaged in an exploration of the topic of wave motion. She often involved the class in whole-group activities as a way to promote conversation and collaboration. During the students' initial conversations about the closely read diagrams, she saw there were learning needs she needed to address. Based on these insights, Ms. Rosen moved from whole-group to small-group instruction. Her actions illustrate very well the process of using formative assessment during close reading instruction.

Using Formative Assessment to Build Close Reading Skill

As we know, close reading involves students returning to a text passage to study language and ideas presented at the word, sentence, paragraph, and passage level, which requires sustained interest and energy on the part of the reader. Of course, closely reading a text also empowers the reader to comprehend, critique, and evaluate ideas within and across texts, resulting in the acquisition of an informed base of knowledge that the reader can use to take a stance and present an enlightened opinion or argument.

This is the goal we are working toward, of course, but students develop this facility over time, and the teacher has a vital role to play in scaffolding students' close reading efforts in order to support forward momentum. As Vygotsky (1978) reminds us, the scaffolding of instruction by a knowledgeable teacher helps a learner build new or extended knowledge from that learner's existing base of knowledge. The scaffolds we provide should be temporary, and as the knowledge of the learner increases, so should learning independence. The overall goal of scaffolding is to help students become independent, self-regulating learners and problem solvers who understand how to advance their own learning.

Think now about how closely this goal parallels the goal of teaching students to analyze complex texts. Teaching them to closely read a text means teaching them to think deeply about the text message by engaging in dialogue or conversation with the author as a means to determine the message and the author's intent in sharing the message. It empowers students to be critical thinkers and independent seekers and creators of understanding.

Let's look an example of how 2nd grade teacher Dan Ramirez developed these skills, pushing his students back into a text to identify an author's intent. The text was *Bats: Creatures of the Night*, a Common Core text exemplar written by Joyce Milton, and the close reading session was part of a unit of study addressing a Next Generation Science Standard (2-LS4-1): "Make observations of plants and animals to compare the diversity of life in different habitats." Using Milton's book as a starting point, Mr. Ramirez asked students to think about this general understanding question: *What about a bat's life is different from the life of other animals, like a dog?* Students listened to Mr. Ramirez read aloud the first close reading as they read along on their printed copies. They annotated the text with colored pencils as Mr. Ramirez had taught them to do. Cedella used a blue pencil to note information about where bats live. After underlining the phrase *sleeping in the loft*, she drew a line to the margin and wrote, "Live here." After the first reading, Mr. Ramirez paused for partner chats, saying, "Talk with your table-mates about what makes the life of a bat different from the life of other animals."

Robert, partnered with Cedella, pointed to the text: "Bats live where no one else lives and they sleep a lot. That's what it says right here." Then Cedella added, "They're also different because they are flying animals that have fur."

By listening in on student talk, Mr. Ramirez realized no one had pointed out the passage addressing bats' nocturnal nature. Was it possible they were not familiar with the concept of *nocturnal?* He hadn't identified this as a potential area of confusion, but he saw now that it needed to be addressed. To help spot-light this concept, Mr. Ramirez paused to have students develop Frayer cards for the term (see Figure 6.2 for an example). They used online dictionaries and infor-mation from a website to create their cards.

Then Mr. Ramirez returned the students to the bat text with this text-dependent question focused on finding key details: *Is there any evidence that lets you know if bats are nocturnal or not?* Now that students had the background vocabulary knowledge they needed, they reread the text for evidence. During

Figure 6.2 | **Frayer Word Card Used in Close Reading of Milton's *Bats***

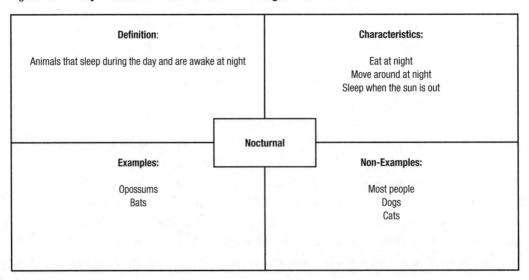

table partner talk, Steven showed Sharon this line: *As the sun goes down, they take to the air.* "As the sun goes down," Steven repeated, adding, "I think bats are nocturnal. That's why they fly at night, when the sun's going down."

Based on the content of this and other student conversations, Mr. Ramirez was satisfied that they understood the concept of *nocturnal.* Next, he sent students back into the text to reread independently and address the final text-dependent question: *Does the author provide strong evidence to show that bats are nocturnal?*

As students continued reading and annotating, Mr. Ramirez noticed that Cedella was numbering her evidence, writing notes above each line of the text that supported the notion that bats are nocturnal. During the follow-up chat session with her tablemates, she clearly outlined her evidence by quoting from the text: "One—*bats take to the air at night.* Two—*they spend most of the time in the dark.* Three—*they catch insects at night.*"

As this example shows, even young students—here, 2nd graders—are able to critique the contents of informational text to seek substantial evidence to support a concept or opinion if they are provided with scaffolded instruction that emerges from continuous formative assessment during the instructional sequence. (For students who struggle with the reading level or the length of the text, repeated read-alouds conducted by the teacher may be more appropriate.) Mr. Ramirez's questions prompted his students to think deeply about the language the author used. His discussion validated that they had existing knowledge of the topic or newly acquired knowledge, but he cautioned them to think about the author's position and not let their prior knowledge overshadow the author's message. What they needed to do, he explained, was seek out text-based evidence. With such a sophisticated academic foundation, Mr. Ramirez's students will be ready for the increased demands of close reading and argumentative essay writing as they move into middle and high school.

Adjusting Close Reading Instruction in Light of Formative Data

Consider the following example of how teacher insights acquired through teacher-and-student conversations during close reading can lead to beneficial instructional adjustments that help achieve learning goals. Notice specifically how the whole-class questions relate so closely to the teachers' identified learning target. Also notice the individual discussion moves that each teacher makes through the questions they ask and the prompts and clues they offer to both individual students and the whole class. In doing so, they backfill the language and background information students need to read successfully. They support students' success during the close reading.

Two 3rd grade teachers, Dennis Perez and Karen Haas, co-planned a close reading session focused on the following passage from Jim LaMarche's *The Raft*[*] (a Common Core text exemplar):

> Somehow, on the river, it seemed like summer would never end. But of course it did.
>
> On my last day, I got up extra early and crept down to the dock. The air was cool and a low pearly fog hung over the river. I untied the raft and quietly drifted downstream.
>
> Ahead of me, through the fog, I saw two deer moving across the river, a doe and a fawn. When they reached the shore, the doe leaped easily up the steep bank, then turned to wait for her baby. But the fawn was in trouble. It kept slipping down the muddy bank. The doe returned to the water to help, but the more the fawn struggled, the deeper it got stuck in the mud.
>
> I pushed off the river bottom and drove the raft hard onto the muddy bank, startling the doe. Then I dropped into the water. I was ankle-deep in mud.
>
> "You're okay," I whispered to the fawn, praying that the raft would calm it. "I won't hurt you."
>
> Gradually the fawn stopped struggling, as if it understood that I was there to help. I put my arms around it and pulled. It barely moved. I pulled again, then again. Slowly the fawn eased out of the mud, and finally it was free. Carefully I carried the fawn up the bank to its mother.
>
> Then, quietly, I returned to the raft. From there I watched the doe nuzzle and clean her baby, and I knew what I had to do. I pulled the stub of a crayon from my pocket, and drew the fawn, in all its wildness, onto the old gray boards of the raft. When I had finished, I knew it was just right.

Each teacher's classroom had a similar composition of students, with a range of language and proficiency levels. Both were addressing the Common Core's Reading Anchor Standard 1 (see p. 172). The grade-level version of this standard in the Literature domain states that 3rd graders students should be able to

---

[*] From *The Raft* (pp. 25–30) by Jim LaMarche, 2000. New York: HarperCollins Publishers. Copyright © 2000 by HarperCollins Publishers. Reprinted with permission.

RL 3.1. Ask and answer questions to demonstrate understanding of a text, referring explicitly to the text as the basis for the answers.

In their pre-planning, Mr. Perez and Mrs. Haas established the following as their lesson purpose: *Understand how the story's setting changed Nicky.* Together, they designed an instructional plan built on students asking and answering questions in order to arrive at this understanding.

As you can see in Figure 6.3's side-by-side comparison of the teachers' instructional plans, they agreed on a common set of text-dependent questions. But as you can also see, Mrs. Haas went on to make significant adjustments to her instruction in light of the formative assessment data she collected during the actual close reading session. While asking text-dependent questions and listening closely to student responses, she determined that some of the questions she had planned could be eliminated because her students already understood the text quite well and didn't need them as scaffolds. For example, when students responded to the second question after the second reading (*What language does the author use to help you visualize the setting?*) with specific words that described the setting (*cool air, muddy bank along the river, fog hanging over the river*), she knew that she didn't need to ask any other text-dependent questions connecting author's language and the setting.

By contrast, what Mr. Perez heard in his students' responses to the very first text-dependent question helped him determine that all of his planned text-dependent questions would be useful; they would provide direction and support that his students needed with a text that turned out to be very challenging for them—a true stretch. He even added a new question (#7 in the figure) because it was clear from students' pattern of responses that they would benefit from another specific example of the way the author used language to evoke setting. Mr. Perez even stepped in to read the text aloud at a certain point, when it was clear that a large number of students were unable to stay focused on it during independent reading. Remember, multiple readings by teachers and peers can be a valuable scaffold for many students.

Formative assessment involves attending not just to what students say in response to text-dependent questions but also attending to whether or how well students manage to attend to the reading. Every behavior that the students exhibit offers insights into their comprehension of the text. Off-task behaviors and text margins filled with doodles rather than on-task notes should also be indicators that provide insights about the appropriate instructional path for each student.

Figure 6.3 | **A Comparison of Formative Assessment Adjustments During a Close Reading**

Mr. Perez's Plan		Mrs. Haas's Plan	
Reading	**Text-Dependent Questions**	**Reading**	**Text-Dependent Questions**
First Reading: Students Read Independently *Many kids looked lost during the reading...few replies to this question.*	1. What is this passage about?	**First Reading:** Students Read Independently	1. What is this passage about?
Second Reading: Students Read Independently	2. What language does the author use to help you visualize the setting? 3. What words does the author use to describe the river on the last morning of the summer?	**Second Reading:** Students Read Independently *Skip question because students shared specific words to describe the setting after the question above. This question wasn't needed.*	2. What language does the author use to help you visualize the setting? 3. ~~What words does the author use to describe the river on the last morning of the summer?~~
Third Reading: Students Read Independently *Read aloud because students' comprehension is breaking down due to their disfluent reading.* *Add question because students needed specific examples on which to focus.*	4. What was Nicky like at the beginning of the story? What is he like at the end? 5. How does the story's setting change Nicky? 6. What words that the author uses to describe the setting help you understand Nicky's transformation? 7. What do we learn about Nicky when the author writes, "I watched the doe nuzzle and clean her baby"?	**Third Reading:** Students Read Independently *Skip because students completely described the characters' transformation.*	4. What was Nicky like at the beginning of the story? What is he like at the end? 5. ~~How does the story's setting change Nicky?~~ 6. What words that the author uses to describe the setting help you understand Nicky's transformation?

Beyond Classroom Assessment of Close Reading: Summative and Formative Measures in the Common Core Assessments

As noted in the Introduction, at press time, plans are in place for students in most of the United States to be tested on their mastery of the Common Core standards via assessments developed by one of two Common Core assessment consortia: the Smarter Balanced Assessment Consortium (Smarter Balanced) or the Partnership for Assessment of Readiness for College and Careers (PARCC). Both consortia plan to assess students in grades 3–8 and in grade 11 using an online assessment that includes a variety of item types: selected responses, constructed responses, and complex performance tasks. These assessments will be administered in the final weeks of the school year, and will employ both electronic and human scoring, and it is projected that teachers will receive their students' results within two weeks of test administration. These results are intended to serve as a summative assessment of the year's learning and provide teachers, students, and families with valid and reliable data on student proficiency levels. Many states have announced plans to use the summative data as a measure of teacher effectiveness, and individual teachers might also use these results to reflect on the effectiveness of their teaching practices and help them identify focus areas for the following year. Educators will also be able to compare student proficiency levels and achievement growth among schools, districts, and states.

Both Smarter Balanced and PARCC also plan to provide optional interim assessments that can be administered throughout the year to generate formative data teachers can use to plan more effective instruction. They can examine student scores to determine which standards need more attention and which areas of instruction need more explicit teaching and scaffolding. The idea is that if a teacher's students do not do well on assessment items that asked them to use details from the text to support answers, the teacher needs to explicitly teach the processes of revisiting text, annotating it, and using a graphic organizer to become more proficient at identifying text-supported evidence.

One of the major differences between the two consortia is that PARCC uses a fixed-form delivery, while Smarter Balanced uses adaptive delivery, meaning students will see an individually tailored set of items and tasks. The adaptive delivery system presents the student with the next assessment question based on the response to the question just answered. Students who answer satisfactorily will get more challenging questions or move on to different aspects of the assessment. Students who answer unsatisfactorily will get more questions with the same level of challenge or less. The intention is that all students, through the answering of text-dependent questions, will be building a base of knowledge, language, and reading skill that will allow the complexity of the texts they read to increase. This adaptive system is a form of formative assessment in that the series of questions to which a student responds is individualized based on his responses.

Starting in 2015–16, PARCC assessments will also include a locally scored, non-summative speaking and listening test intended to provide students opportunities to demonstrate skills they need to perform successfully at school and will later need in workplace situations. Students will show off their speaking and listening prowess through both real-time engagement and assessments for which they can do advanced preparation. The Real-Time performance assessments, administered in grades 3, 5, 7, 9, and 11, will involve students listening to prerecorded speeches and media productions and then spontaneously responding to related questions. The Advanced Preparation assessments, administered in grades 4, 6, 8, 10, and 12, give students time to conduct research on authentic topics and then require them to give a formal spoken presentation of their findings (assessing speaking skills) and respond spontaneously to questions from the audience (assessing both listening and speaking skills). The teachers who will be scoring these speaking and listening assessments will be cautioned to be sensitive to presentations by English language learners and students with disabilities; dialects or "mispronunciations" that diverge from the standard academic register are not to be viewed as errors. In addition to using the data from these interim assessments in a formative manner to inform decisions about the speaking and listening instruction and opportunities students will receive in classrooms, teachers might also use them in assigning grades. The instructional scenarios included in Chapter 5 provide examples that can help you support the speaking and listening skill development of your students.

Both assessment consortia pledge to provide information that is helpful in determining school effectiveness, directions for teaching, learning and program improvement, and individual student college and career readiness.

Making "Big" Summative Assessments Useful in the Classroom

Teachers have often been concerned that their students' scores on state and national assessments do not connect to their classroom instruction, either because the data from these assessments do not reach teachers in a timely fashion or because the data are in a format that does not identify the specific areas in which a student needs support. This concern has not gone unnoticed. The SAT, a high-stakes summative college admissions assessment, is being redesigned to more closely reflect what is being taught in schools. According to David Coleman, president of the College Board, the present reading and writing items on the SAT will be replaced with source materials "important for educated Americans to know and understand deeply" and test items that require students to provide evidence and justification for their responses (Balf, 2014, p. 31).

The historical lack of usefulness of national test results highlights a mismatch between the intent of the assessments and teachers' intended uses of the results. Teachers generally want assessment data they can use to focus on student response as a way to monitor and further plan instruction. This is what formative assessment data collected during any type of instruction, including close reading instruction, has the potential to give us: immediate and continual feedback on students' ability to analyze complex text and access the content of the discipline. This information is so useful in daily instructional planning. When you are creating an assessment task to use in association with a close reading session or formulating the text-dependent questions you plan to use, always ask yourself this key question: *How will students' responses inform my instructional planning, reveal the progress they are making, and point me toward the instructional interventions I may need to make?*

That said, summative assessment items on large-scale assessments can also be useful in instructional planning. We recommend taking a look at the large depository of sample assessment items and performance tasks that SBAC provides at http://sampleitems.smarterbalanced.org/itempreview/sbac/ELA.htm. These items are sortable by grade bands and content focus, and evaluation rubrics are also provided.

Analyzing items associated with the grade or grades you teach not only is a great way to gain insight about the skills that are being assessed and the kind of instruction you need to provide, but it also drives home how close reading will help students develop the skills and stamina they need to read test items critically and analytically. For example, an SBAC sample performance task for evaluating Writing Standard 3 called "Oliver's Big Splash" (Item 43009) asks 4th grade students to read two paragraphs that are "the beginning of a story," revise those paragraphs to provide more detail, and then write an ending to the story. In order to accomplish this writing task, students must read the two paragraphs closely enough to note the sequence of events and the language style the original author used so that it can be matched and extended. This assessment example illustrates the type of reading and writing skills and strategies that students will need to be taught in order to respond accurately to multi-step assessments when they appear on future assessments.

Remember, too, that the Common Core State Standards offer learning progressions for each identified anchor standard—including Reading Anchor Standard 1, which focuses on closely reading informational and literary texts. Although these progressions are not based on research data, it was documented by Pearson (2013), in communication with the developers of the Common Core, that these progressions are based on a consensus of opinion of experts regarding how the identified skills develop. In our view, using an authoritative body of experts to make such decisions is a valid way of establishing such a progression. In fact, as we mentioned in the Introduction, this is pretty similar to how basal reader skill progressions have been established for decades. In Figure 6.4, we share the progression of Reading Anchor Standard 1 from kindergarten through grade 5, along with a few related areas of instructional focus. Also included are examples of sample assessment items similar to those created by Smarter Balanced and PARCC (where applicable) and available in Appendix B of the Common Core ELA/literacy standards document.

What becomes obvious from reviewing the progression of Reading Standard 1 and the test items designed to assess it at the various grade levels is that students are being asked to move beyond the identification of information and to think about and analyze what they are reading. They are being asked to look deeply at a text and to think about what they are reading by explicitly and implicitly considering the language, author intent, text structure, and context.

Download

Figure 6.4 | **Reading Anchor Standard 1: Progression of Instruction and Assessment, Grades K–5**

CCRA.R.1. Read closely to determine what the text says explicitly and to make logical inferences from it; cite specific textual evidence when writing or speaking to support conclusions drawn from the text.

Grade-Level Standard*	Area of Focus—Instructional Possibilities	Examples of Assessment
Kindergarten **RI.K.1.** With prompting and support, ask and answer questions about key details in a text. **RL.K.1.** With prompting and support, ask and answer questions about key details in a text.	Because most kindergarten students will not be able to fluently decode a text, focus on engaging them in listening to a text and craft questions that ask them to identify and discuss key text details. *Sample Informational Text Question:* What happens to the seed in winter? (Ask this for each season.) *Sample Literature Question:* How did the author tell you and show you the events of Toad's day?	*Not assessed through SBAC or PARCC. Sample performance tasks are available in Appendix B of the Common Core's ELA/literacy standards document.* • Students (with prompting and support from the teacher) read *A Tree Is a Plant* by Clyde Robert Bulla and demonstrate their understanding of the main idea of the text—the life cycle of a tree—by retelling key details. • Students (with prompting and support from the teacher) describe the relationship between key events of the overall story of *Frog and Toad Together* by Arnold Lobel, comparing his words and illustrations..
Grade 1 **RI.1.1.** Ask and answer questions about key details in a text. **RL.1.1.** Ask and answer questions about key details in a text.	Because few students in grade 1 will be reading with fluency, focus on getting them to ask and answer questions about the key details of text read aloud. Notice that unlike students in kindergarten, they will be expected to do so without teacher prompting, so focus on building students' ability to ask and answer questions without assistance. *Sample Informational Text Question:* What words and phrases did Edith Thacher Hurd use to describe starfish? How do the illustrations by Robin Brickman show you what Edith Thacher Hurd told you? *Sample Literature Question:* What words and phrases did the author use to describe Mr. Popper?	*Not assessed through SBAC or PARCC. Sample performance tasks are available in Appendix B of the Common Core's ELA/literacy standards document.* • Students use the illustrations and textual details in Edith Thacher Hurd's *Starfish* to describe scientific features of starfish. • Students identify words and phrases within *Mr. Popper's Penguins* by Richard and Florence Atwater that introduce character development in a humorous way.

*Note: In grades K–5, the grade-level standards for CCRA.R.1 are phrased identically in both the Literature and Informational Text domains.

Download

Grade-Level Standard*	Area of Focus—Instructional Possibilities	Examples of Assessment
Grade 2 **RI.2.1.** Ask and answer such questions as who, what, where, when, why, and how to demonstrate understanding of key details in a text. **RL.2.1.** Ask and answer such questions as who, what, where, when, why, and how to demonstrate understanding of key details in a text.	Notice the specificity of the types of questions that 2nd graders should be able to ask and answer. Give students plenty of practice going back to the text to find these kinds of answers. Note that there is no expectation that students be able to read text independently. *Sample Informational Text Question:* What happens to the surface of a drop of water when it shrinks to its smallest size? *Sample Literature Question:* What are some similarities between Ardis the Mermaid and Hemlock?	*Not assessed through SBAC or PARCC. Sample performance tasks are available in Appendix B of the Common Core's ELA/literacy standards document.* • Students read *A Drop of Water: A Book of Science and Wonder* by Walter Wick, which includes descriptions of water in various forms. Students can demonstrate their understanding of all forms of water by answering who, what, where, when, why, and how text-dependent questions with key details. • Students identify how the characters are developed in *The Search for Delicious* by Natalie Babbitt, which describes Gaylen's travels and the unusual characters he meets.
Grade 3 **RI.3.1.** Ask and answer questions to demonstrate understanding of a text, referring explicitly to the text as the basis for the answers. **RL.3.1.** Ask and answer questions to demonstrate understanding of a text, referring explicitly to the text as the basis for the answers.	By grade 3, students need to be able to cite the part of the text where they found the support for their answers. Although it's not stated explicitly that students in grade 3 must be reading independently, it's implied by the phrase "referring explicitly to the text." Students must show text evidence to support their selection.	PART A What is one main idea of "How Plants Live"? a. There are many types of plants on the planet. b. Plants need water to live. c. There are many ways to sort different plants. d. All plants begin their life cycles in different forms. PART B Which details from the article best support the answer to Part A? a. "Plants don't use oxygen, they create it." b. "Plants can be grouped by their traits." c. "Plants are chlorophytes." d. "All plants grow and change over time." e. "Almost all plants need water, food, oxygen, and shelter to live." *Notice how in order to complete part Part B, the student had to comprehend Part A*

Grade-Level Standard*	Area of Focus—Instructional Possibilities	Examples of Assessment
Grade 4 **RI.4.1.** Refer to details and examples in a text when explaining what the text says explicitly and when drawing inferences from the text. **RLI.4.1.** Refer to details and examples in a text when explaining what the text says explicitly and when drawing inferences from the text.	Here in grade 4, the specificity of what students are asked to do increases. They are now expected to note the text details and examples that support their understanding of not just what the text says explicitly but also what they are able to infer from closely reading a small passage.	What does Anthony learn about Uncle Al from their conversation? Use details from the text to support your answer. Type your answer in the space provided. *Note:* This item asks students to consider a specific subsection of the text and the general topic of that section.
Grade 5 **RI.5.1.** Quote accurately from a text when explaining what the text says explicitly and when drawing inferences from the text. **RL.5.1.** Quote accurately from a text when explaining what the text says explicitly and when drawing inferences from the text.	In grade 5, students must fully engage with the language of the text and quote from it accurately as they explain the inferences they have drawn as the text is closely read.	**Question:** Choose the two main ideas and drag them into the empty box under the heading "Main Ideas." Then choose one detail that best supports each main idea and drag it into the empty box under the heading "Supporting Detail."

Possible Main Ideas	2 Main Ideas	3 Possible Supporting Details	1 Supporting Detail
David has many models of cars.	David is an experienced builder of model cars.	David thinks building model cars is fun.	As a designer of model cars, David has built hundreds throughout his life.
David is an experienced builder of model cars.	David hopes to someday have a model car museum.	David has lots of friends who have collections.	David loves to share his models with others.
David hopes to someday have a model car museum.		David spends most of his allowance on model cars.	
David uses inexpensive materials to build his model cars.		David loves to share his models with others.	

⇒◆⇐

Teaching every student to "read like a detective and write like an investigative reporter" (Coleman, 2011, p. 11) implies a move to the upper quadrants of Bloom's taxonomy and greater emphasis upon analyzing, hypothesizing, and critical evaluation. As Petrilli and Finn (2010) note, "Standards describe the destination that schools and students are supposed to reach, but by themselves have little power to effect change" (para. 4). The instruction you provide between the identification of the standard and student performance on the new and challenging Common Core assessments is a key determiner how well your students will perform. By engaging students in close reading, you're helping them develop the skills and stamina they need to succeed. Through the process of formative assessment that we have shared in this chapter, you can focus on the immediate performance of your students during close reading and, based on what you observe, provide them with the instructional scaffolds they need to be able to read and learn from a complex text.

CONCLUSION

Like you, we realize that implementing the Common Core State Standards is a major undertaking that requires a reexamination of instruction. The ideas and examples presented in this text are shared to help you better understand what's involved in teaching your students to closely read a text, and to support you in accommodating this added feature of instruction within your already crowded instructional day.

Just think for a minute about all that you already know about how to teach your students to read and communicate about texts. Don't let go of this information! Now add to those many research-supported practices one new practice—engaging your students in closely reading a short text or text segment.

As you have come to realize through your close reading of this book, the practice of close reading gets students involved in analyzing text-based information at a word, phrase, paragraph, or whole-passage level. While they are doing so, they make decisions about how all of the information fits together. They determine the central themes, ideas, contrasting perspectives, validity of arguments, and why the author chose this specific language to present the information. The thinking that students engage in during a close reading parallels the thinking we all do to succeed in daily life, as we're barraged with information from a wide variety of sources. What should be believed, repeated, studied, investigated, challenged, or disregarded? We can only make these decisions if we are able to think analytically.

Close reading instruction provides you the opportunity to teach your students to analyze complex text. Your questions cause them to return to the message of the text to determine its important ideas, and the facts and documentation supporting those ideas. Your questions help them to note similarities and differences across texts, to synthesize information, to evaluate the veracity of an author's claim, and to grasp the power of language. With your perseverance, they can learn to think deeply about information shared in the messages they receive in both written and spoken forms. With practice attending to these details, your students will eventually be able to engage in closely reading texts and doing all of this analysis independently. Just as you taught them to read, you will now teach them to closely read. The skills of analysis they gain from close text scrutiny will also empower their written and spoken discourses as they study an issue from multiple perspectives, and then share and support a well-grounded stance.

As a teacher, you are committed to providing the best possible instruction for each of your students. You continually add new practices to your instructional toolbox. Close reading instruction is one such practice. It can and should be used in all subject areas, and in all kinds of instructional configurations: whole class and small group. It's a complex undertaking with a simple-to-describe format: students read a complex text multiple times, guided by text-dependent questions and subsequent discussions that take them deeper into the text, where they develop a nuanced understanding of the text's information and language, as well as the author's intent. As you continue to implement the practice of close reading over time, you will see your students becoming increasingly able to tackle more difficult texts on their own. You will have given them vital tools that will serve them well as they move into middle school, high school, and beyond—into college and careers and the next steps of their lives.

We hope we have helped you gain a better understanding of the process of close reading, its purpose, and all that students have to gain from its use. Give close reading a try in your classroom, and you'll be amazed, as we were, at how it will empower the thinking and communicating your students do.

APPENDIX A

A GUIDE FOR ADMINISTRATORS

How to Support Whole-School Implementaton of Close Reading

- Become informed about text complexity and close reading by learning what the Common Core Standards say about these important topics.
- Schedule and attend workshops for your teachers that demonstrate how to analyze texts for text complexity and how to do close reading.
- Give teachers time for whole-school planning for close reading, identifying key goals and coordinating (1) what texts will be used at different grade levels, and (2) how close reading will be integrated into language arts, social studies, science, and mathematics.
- Give teachers time for grade-level planning for close reading to determine schedules for close reading experiences during each school day.
- Work with teachers to decide upon schoolwide or grade-level annotations so students do not need to relearn annotation markings each year.
- Provide coaching for teachers as they "try on" close reading in their classrooms.
- Support teachers' efforts to implement close reading by arranging opportunities for peer observation and feedback.
- Use an observation form that parallels the planning they are doing for close reading instruction. An example follows on pages 178–181.

A CLOSE READING OBSERVATION GUIDE

Teacher: _____ Observer: _____

Grade: _____ Date: _____ Time: _____

Text Title: _____ ○ Whole Group ○ Small Group

○ Purpose statement is posted and explained.
○ Short complex passage is used.
○ Passage is numbered.
○ Annotation chart is posted, and students are annotating text.
○ Passage is read multiple times, as indicated below. Rereading the text 3–4 times is typical, but not required

	1st read	2nd read	3rd read	4th read
Teacher				
Students				

○ Frontloading is limited.
○ Teacher asks text-dependent questions.
○ Partner talk is used.
○ Writing or closing task extends meaning or is used for assessment purposes.

Questions to Consider:

• Is the purpose addressed throughout the lesson?
• What text-dependent questions are asked?

• How is partner talk used to enhance students' understanding?
• Are insights gained from students' responses used to scaffold follow-up questions, discussion, and instruction?

1st Reading Notes/ Comments:

2nd Reading
Notes/Comments:

3rd Reading Notes/
Comments:

**4th Reading Notes/
Comments:**

**Focus Forward
Notes:**

Resources for Learning More

Online

- EngageNY (www.engageny.org) is a comprehensive website for educators from the New York State Education Department that contains videos, professional development modules and resources, information for students and parents, and more.
- EduCore: Tools for Teaching the Common Core (http://educore.ascd.org/) from ASCD contains resources for teachers and administrators that include evidence-based strategies, videos, and supporting documents designed to support educators as they transition to the Common Core State Standards.
- The National Association of Elementary School Principals (NAESP) has a section of their website called Common Core State Standards Resources (www.naesp.org/common-core-state-standards-resources) featuring resources for teachers and administrators related to the Common Core, including an implementation checklist and action briefs designed to provide information about the standards.
- The International Reading Association (www.reading.org) has numerous resources related to implementation of the English language arts standards that include webinars featuring experts in literacy instruction.
- The Text Project (http://textproject.org/professional-development/) contains Common Core–related resources for teachers and administrators, including information on text complexity and free webinars on a range of topics related to the standards.

Books

- Calkins, L., Ehrenworth, M., & Lehman, C. (2012). *Pathways to the Common Core: Accelerating achievement.* Portsmouth, NH: Heinemann.
- Fisher, D., Frey, N., & Lapp, D. (2012). *Text complexity: Raising rigor in reading.* Newark, DE: International Reading Association.

APPENDIX B

COMMON CORE TEXT EXEMPLAR LOCATOR

You can find (and read) excerpts of the Common Core text exemplars discussed in this book in Appendix B to the Common Core State Standards for English Language Arts & Literacy in History/Social Studies, Science, and Technical Subjects. This document is available online at **http://www.corestandards.org/assets/ Appendix_B.pdf.**

The excerpts are the perfect length for close reading.

Title & Author	Location in the CCSS Appendix B	Text Type & Genre	Grade Band
Alice's Adventures in Wonderland; Lewis Carroll	p. 63	Literature: Story	4–5
Amos & Boris; William Steig	p. 38	Literature: Story	2–3
Are You My Mother?; P. D. Eastman	p. 15	Literature: Story	K–1
Bat Loves the Night; Nicola Davies	p. 56	Informational Text: Literary Nonfiction	2–3
Bats Creatures of the Night; Joyce Milton	p. 54	Informational Text: Literary Nonfiction	2–3
The Black Stallion; Walter Farley	p. 64	Literature: Story	4–5
The Birchbark House; Louise Erdrich	p. 65	Literature: Story	4–5
Bud, Not Buddy; Christopher Curtis	p. 65	Literature: Story	4–5
"By Myself"; Eloise Greenfield	p. 18	Literature: Poem	K–1
Charlotte's Web; E. B. White	p. 47	Literature: Story	2–3
Cowgirl Kate and Cocoa; Erica Silverman	p. 42	Literature: Story	2–3
Discovering Mars: The Amazing Story of the Red Planet; Melvin Berger	p. 70	Informational Text: Expository Text	2–3
A Drop of Water: A Book of Science and Wonder; Walter Wick	p.58	Informational Text: Expository Text	2–3
Earthworms; Claire Llewellyn	p. 33	Informational Text: Expository Text	K–1
Family Pictures; Carmen Lomas Garza	p. 23	Literature: Story	K–1

Title & Author	Location in the CCSS Appendix B	Text Type & Genre	Grade Band
The Fire Cat; Esther Averill	p. 37	Literature: Story	2–3
"Fireflies"; Paul Fleischman	p. 52	Literature: Poem	2–3
Frog and Toad Together; Arnold Lobel	p. 15	Literature: Story	K–1
From Seed to Pumpkin; Wendy Pfeffer	p. 33	Informational Text: Expository & Procedural Text	K–1
Garden Helpers; National Geographic Young Explorers	p. 31	Informational Text: Literary Nonfiction/ Digital Text	K–1
Henry and Mudge: The First Book of Their Adventures; Cynthia Rylant	p. 39	Literature: Story	2–3
History of US: Liberty for All?; Joy Hakim	p. 72	Informational Text: Literary Nonfiction	4–5
Horses; Seymour Simon	p. 40	Informational Text: Expository Text	4–5
Hurricanes: Earth's Mightiest Storms; Patricia Lauber	p. 71	Informational Text: Expository Text	4–5
If the World Were a Village: A Book About the World's People; David Smith	p. 59	Informational Text: Expository Text	2–3
The Lighthouse Family: The Storm; Cynthia Rylant	p. 41	Literature: Story	2–3
Lincoln: A Photobiography; Russell Friedman	p. 57	Informational Text: Literary nonfiction	2–3
Little Bear; Else Holmelund Minarik	p. 14	Literature: Story	K–1
The Little Prince; Antoine de Saint-Exúpery	p. 64	Literature: Story	4–5
"Living Fences" in *England: The Land;* Erinn Banting	p. 72	Informational Text: Expository Text	4–5
M.C. Higgins, the Great; Virginia Hamilton	p. 64	Literature: Story	4–5
Moonshot: The Flight of Apollo 11; Brian Floca	p. 56	Informational Text: Literary Nonfiction	2–3
Mr. Popper's Penguins; Richard and Florence Atwater	p. 21	Literature: Story	K–1
My Librarian Is a Camel: How Books Are Brought to Children Around the World; Margriet Ruurs	p. 72	Informational Text: Expository Text	4–5
"The New Colossus"; Emma Lazarus	p. 67	Literature: Poem	4–5
"The Owl and the Pussycat"; Edward Lear	p. 27	Literature: Poem	K–1
Owl at Home; Arnold Lobel	p. 16	Literature: Story	K–1

Continued ➜

Title & Author	Location in the CCSS Appendix B	Text Type & Genre	Grade Band
Poppleton in Winter; Cynthia Rylant	p. 40	Literature: Story	2–3
Quest for the Tree Kangaroo: An Expedition into the Cloud Forest of New Guinea; Sy Montgomery	p. 73	Informational Text: Expository Text	4–5
The Raft; Jim LaMarche	p. 73	Literature: Story	2–3
Sarah, Plain and Tall; Patricia MacLachlan	p. 38	Literature: Story	2–3
The Search for Delicious; Natalie Babbitt	p. 48	Literature: Story	2–3
The Secret Garden; Frances Hodgson Burnett	p. 63	Literature: Story	4–5
"Seeing Eye to Eye"; Leslie Hall	p. 74	Informational Text: Expository Text	4–5
Starfish; Edith Thacher Hurd	p. 30	Informational Text: Literary Nonfiction	K–1
"Stopping by Woods on a Snowy Evening"; Robert Frost	p. 44	Literature: Poem	2–3
A Story, a Story; Gail E. Haley	p. 21	Literature: Story	K–1
The Story of Ruby Bridges; Robert Coles	p. 58	Informational Text: Literary Nonfiction	2–3
"They Were My People"; *Grace Nichols*	p. 69	Literature: Poem	4–5
Tomas and the Library Lady; Pat Mora	p. 23	Literature: Story	K–1
Tops and Bottoms; Janet Stevens	p. 40	Literature: Story	2–3
A Tree Is a Plant; Clyde Robert Bulla	p. 28	Informational Texts Literary Nonfiction	K–1
Tuck Everlasting; Natalie Babbitt	p. 64	Literature: Story	4–5
"Underground Railroad" in *Flight to Freedom;* Henrietta Buckmaster	p. 76	Informational Text: Literary Nonfiction	4–5
Volcanoes; Seymour Simon	p. 74	Informational Text: Expository Text	4–5
Water, Water, Everywhere; Mark Rauzon & Cynthia Overbeck Bix	p. 33	Informational Text: Expository Text	K–1
We Are the Ship: The Story of Negro League Baseball; Kadir Nelson	p. 74	Informational Text: Literary Nonfiction	2–3
Where Do Polar Bears Live?; Sarah L. Thomson	p. 57	Informational Text: Literary Nonfiction	2–3
Where the Mountain Meets the Moon; Grace Lin	p. 66	Literature: Story	4–5
A Wrinkle in Time; Madeleine L'Engle	p. 79	Literature: Story	4–5
Zin! Zin! Zin! A Violin; Lloyd Moss	p. 27	Literature: Story	K–1

REFERENCES

Achieve, College Summit, National Association of Secondary School Principals [NASSP] & National Association of Elementary School Principals [NAESP]. (2013). *Implementing the common core state standards: The role of the secondary school leader.* Retrieved from www.achieve.org/files/RevisedSecondaryActionBrief_Final_Feb.pdf

ACT. (2006). Reading between the lines: What the ACT reveals about college readiness in reading. Iowa City, IA: Author. Available: www.act.org/research/policymakers/pdf/reading_summary.pdf

Adams, M. J. (2010–2011, Winter). Advancing our students' language and literacy: The challenge of complex texts. *American Educator, 34*(4), 3–12.

Adler, M. J., & Van Doren, C. (1940/1972). *How to read a book.* New York: Touchstone.

Anderson, L. W., Krathwohl, D. R., Airasian, P. W., Cruikshank, K. A., Mayer, R. E., Pintrich, P. R., Raths, J., & Wittrock, M. C. (2001). *A taxonomy for learning, teaching, and assessing: A revision of Bloom's taxonomy of educational objectives* (Complete ed.). New York: Longman.

Anderson, R. C., & Pearson, P. D. (1984). A schema-theoretic view of basic processes in reading comprehension. In P. D. Pearson (Ed.), *Handbook of reading research* (pp. 255–291). New York: Longman.

Atwater, R., & Atwater, F. (1992). *Mr. Popper's penguins* (Reissue ed.). New York: Little, Brown Books for Young Readers.

Balf, T. (2014, March 9). The SAT is hated by . . . all of the above. *The New York Times Magazine,* 28–31, 48–51.

Bauerline, M. (2011, February). Too dumb for complex texts? *Educational Leadership, 68*(5), 28–33.

Black, P., & Wiliam, D. (1998). Inside the black box: Raising standards through classroom assessment. *Phi Delta Kappan, 80*(2), 139–148.

Bloom, B. S. (Ed.), Engelhart, M. D., Furst, E. J., Hill, W. H., & Krathwohl, D. R. (1956). *Taxonomy of educational objectives: The classification of educational goals. Handbook 1: Cognitive domain.* New York: David McKay.

Brown, W. S. (2011). *Supporting students in a time of core standards: Grades 9–12.* Urbana, IL: National Council of Teachers of English.

Buell, D. (2009). *Classroom strategies for interactive learning* (3rd ed.). Newark, DE: International Reading Association.

Burkins, J., & Yaris, K. (2012, May 18). The centrality of text [blog post]. Retrieved from http://www.burkinsandyaris.com/the-centrality-of-text/

Calkins, L., Ehrenworth, M., & Lehman, C. (2012). *Pathways to the Common Core: Accelerating achievement.* Portsmouth, NH: Heinemann.

Caswell, L. J., & Duke, N. K. (1998). Non-narratives as a catalyst for literacy development. *Language Arts, 75,* 108–117.

Cervetti, G., Paradeles, M. J., & Damico, J. S. (n.d.). A tale of differences: Comparing the traditions, perspectives, and educational goal of critical reading and critical literacy. Retrieved from http://www.readingonline.org/articles/art_index.asp?HREF=/articles/cervetti/index.html

Chall, J., & Jacobs, V. (2003, Spring). The classic study on poor children's fourth-grade slump. *American Educator, 27*(1). Available: http://www.aft.org/newspubs/periodicals/ae/spring2003/hirschsbclassic.cfm

Chall, J., Jacobs, V., & Baldwin, L. (1990). *The reading crisis: Why poor children fall behind.* Cambridge, MA: Harvard University Press.

Cody, A. (2013, November 16). Common core standards: 10 colossal errors. [blog post]. Retrieved from http://blogs.edweek.org/teachers/living-in-dialogue/2013/11/common_core_standards_ten_colo.html

Coiro, J., & Dobler, E. (2007). Exploring the online comprehension strategies used by sixth grade skilled readers to search for and locate information on the Internet. *Reading Research Quarterly, 42,* 214–257.

Coleman, D. (2011, April 28). Bringing the Common Core to life [webinar transcript]. Retrieved from http://usny.nysed.gov/rttt/resources/bringing-the-common-core-to-life.html

Coleman, D., & Pimentel, S. (2012). *Revised publishers' criteria for the Common Core State Standards in English language arts and literacy, grades 3–12.* Washington, DC: National Governors Association Center for Best Practices and Council of Chief State School Officers. Available: http://www.corestandards.org/assets/Publishers_Criteria_for_3-12.pdf

Common Core. (2012). *The Common Core curriculum maps: English language arts grades K–5.* Jossey Bass: San Francisco.

Common Core State Standards Initiative. (2014). *Key shifts in English language arts.* Retrieved from http://www.corestandards.org/other-resources/key-shifts-in-english-language-arts/

Copeland, M. (2005). *Socratic circles: Fostering critical and creative thinking in middle and high school.* Portland, ME: Stenhouse.

Cornell, B. (2000, October 16). Families: Pulling the plug on TV. Retrieved from http://content.time.com/time/magazine/article/0,9171,998244,00.html

Cunningham, J. (1982). Generating interactions between schemata and text. In J. A. Niles and L. A. Harris (Eds.), *New inquiries in reading research and instruction* (pp. 42–47). Washington, DC: National Reading Conference.

Duke, N. K. (2000). 3.6 minutes per day: The scarcity of informational texts in first grade. *Reading Research Quarterly, 35,* 202–224.

Duke, N. K., & Bennett-Armistead, S. (2003). *Reading and writing informational texts in the primary grades.* New York: Scholastic.

Duke, N. K., Caughlan, S., Juzwik, M., & Martin, N. (2011). *Reading and writing genre with purpose in K–8 classrooms.* Portsmouth, NH: Heinemann.

Duke, N. K., & Roberts, K. L. (2010). The genre-specific nature of reading comprehension. In D. Wyse, R. Andrews, and J. Hoffman (Eds.), *The Routledge International Handbook of English, Language and Literacy Teaching* (pp.74–86). London: Routledge.

Duncan, A. (2014, January 27). Seize the day: Change in the classroom and the core of schooling. Remarks at the ASCD Leadership Institute Conference, Washington, DC. Available: http://www.ed.gov/news/speeches/seize-day-change-classroom-and-core-schooling

Fearn, L., & Farnan, N. (2001). *Interactions: Teaching writing and the language arts.* Boston: Houghton Mifflin.

Finton, N. (2004). *Earth science: Wonders of water. National Geographic reading expeditions.* Washington, DC: National Geographic Society.

Fisher, D., & Frey, N. (2014). *Common core: English language arts in a PLC at work, grades 3–5.* Bloomington, IN: Solution Tree.

Fisher, D., Frey, N., & Lapp, D. (2012). *Text complexity: Raising rigor in reading.* Newark, DE: International Reading Association.

Frey, N., & Fisher, D. (2011). *The formative assessment action plan: Practical steps to more successful teaching and learning.* Alexandria, VA: ASCD.

George, J. (1997). *Everglades.* New York: HarperCollins.

Grant, M., Lapp, D., Fisher, D., Johnson, K., & Frey, N. (2012). Purposeful instruction: Mixing up the "I," "we," and "you." *Journal of Adolescent and Adult Literacy, 56*(1), 45–55.

Guthrie, J. T., Schafer, W. D., Von Secker, C., & Alban, T. (2000). Contributions of integrated reading instruction and text resources to achievement and engagement in a statewide school improvement program. *Journal of Educational Research, 93,* 211–26.

Guthrie, J., & Wigfield, A. (2000). Engagement and motivation in reading. In M. Kamil, P. Mosenthal, D. Pearson, and R. Barr (Eds.), *Handbook of reading research* (pp. 518–533). Mahwah, NJ: Erlbaum.

Hakim, J. (2007). *A history of US: Liberty for all? 1820–1860* (3rd rev. ed. *A History of US Book Five*). New York: Oxford University Press.

Hall, L. (2009, September). Seeing eye to eye. *National Geographic Explorer.*

Hart, B., & Risley, T. (1995). *Meaningful differences in the everyday experience of young American children.* Baltimore MD: Brookes.

Hattie, J., & Timperley, H. (2007). The power of feedback. *Review of Educational Research, 77*(1), 81–112.

Hunt Institute. (2011, August 19). *Literacy in other disciplines* [video file]. Retrieved from http://www.youtube.com/watch?v=1zHWMfg_8r0

Hutten, S. (2013). No fear. *The source: California History-Social Science Quarterly Magazine,* 5. Retrieved from http://chssp.ucdavis.edu/source-magazine/teaching-the-common-core

Ivey, G. (2010, March). Texts that matter. *Educational Leadership, 67*(6), 18–23.

Jeong, J., Gaffney, J. S., & Choi, J. (2010). Availability and use of informational texts in second-, third- and fourth-grade classrooms. *Research in the Teaching of English, 44*(4), 435–56.

Joos, M. (1967). *Five clocks.* New York: Harcourt, Brace, & World.

Kamil, M. (2004, August). *Reading to learn 2004.* Paper presented at the Reading to Learn Summer Institute, Escondido, California.

Kamil, M., & Lane, D. (1997). *Using information text for first grade reading instruction: Theory and practice.* Paper presented at the National Reading Conference, Scottsdale, Arizona.

Kuhn, M. R., & Stahl, S. A. (2000). *Fluency: A review of developmental and remedial practices.* Ann Arbor, MI: Center for the Improvement of Early Reading Achievement.

Kulhavy, R. W. (1977). Feedback in written instruction. *Review of Educational Research, 47*(1), 211–232.

LaMarche, J. (2000). *The raft.* New York: HarperCollins Publishers.

Lapp, D., & Fisher, D. (2009). It's all about the book: Motivating teens to read. *Journal of Adolescent & Adult Literacy, 52*(7), 556–651.

Lapp, D., Fisher, D., Flood, J., & Cabello, A. (2001). An integrated approach to the teaching and assessment of language arts. In S. R. Hurley and J. V. Tinajero (Eds.), *Literacy assessment of second language learners* (pp. 1–26). Boston: Allyn & Bacon.

Lapp, D., Grant, M., Moss, B., & Johnson, K. (2013). Students' close reading of science texts: What's now? what's next? *The Reading Teacher, 67*(2), 109–119.

Lee, C. D., & Spratley, A. (2010). *Reading in the disciplines: The challenges of adolescent literacy*. New York: Carnegie Corporation of New York.

Leu, D., Castek, J., Hartman, D., Coiro, J., Henry, L., Kulikowich, J., et al. (2005). *Evaluating the development of scientific knowledge and new forms of reading comprehension during online learning*. Final report presented to the North Central Regional Educational Laboratory/Learning Point Associates. Retrieved from http://newliteracies.uconn.edu/ncrel-grant-project/

Lin, G. (2009). *Where the mountain meets the moon*. New York: Little, Brown Young Readers.

Luke, A., & Freebody, P. (1999). A map of possible practices: Further notes on the four resources model. *Practically Primary, 4*(2), 5–8.

Marinak, B., & Gambrell, L. (2008). Intrinsic motivation and rewards: What sustains young children's engagement with text? *Literacy Research and Instruction, 47*(1), 9–26.

McConachie, S. M., & Petrosky, A. R. (2010). *Content matters: A disciplinary literacy approach to improving student learning*. San Francisco: Jossey Bass.

MetaMetrics. (2014a). Typical reader measures by grade. Retrieved from http://www.lexile.com/about-lexile/grade-equivalent/grade-equivalent-chart

MetaMetrics. (2014b). Typical text measures by grade. Retrieved from http://www.lexile.com/about-lexile/grade-equivalent/grade-equivalent-chart

Miller, R., & Calfee, R. (2004). Comprehending through composing: Reflections on reading assessment strategies. In S. Paris and S. Stahl (Eds.), *Children's Reading Comprehension and Assessment* (pp. 215–233). New York: Routledge.

Mohr, K. (2006). Children's choices for recreational reading: A three-part investigation of selection preferences, rationales, and processes. *Journal of Literacy Research, 38*(1), 81–104.

Moss, B. (2002a). Close up: An interview with Dr. Richard Vacca. *The California Reader, 36*, 54–59.

Moss, B. (2002). *Exploring the literature of fact: Children's nonfiction trade books in the elementary classroom*. New York: Guilford.

Moss, B. (2008). The information text gap: The mismatch between non-narrative text types in basal readers and 2009 NAEP recommended guidelines. *Journal of Literacy Research, 40*, 201–219.

Moss, B. (2011). Boost critical thinking: New titles for thematically based text sets. *Voices from the Middle, 19*(1), 46–48.

National Governors Association [NGA] Center for Best Practices & Council of Chief State School Officers [CCSSO]. (2010a). *Common Core State Standards for English language arts and literacy in history/social studies, science, and technical subjects*. Washington, DC: Authors. Retrieved from www.corestandards.org/assets/CCSSI_ELA%20Standards.pdf

National Governors Association [NGA] Center for Best Practices & Council of Chief State School Officers [CCSSO]. (2010b). *Common Core State Standards for English language arts & literacy in history/social studies, science, and technical subjects—Appendix B: Text exemplars and sample performance tasks*. Washington, DC: Authors.

NGS Lead States. (2013). Next Generation Science Standards. Retrieved from http://www.nextgenscience.org/next-generation-science-standards

Palincsar, A. S., & Duke, N. K. (2004). The role of text and text-reader interactions in young children's reading development and achievement. *The Elementary School Journal, 105*(2), 183–197.

Pappas, C. C. (1993). Is narrative "primary"? Some insights from kindergartners' pretend readings of stories and information books. *Journal of Reading Behavior, 25*, 97–129.

Partnership for Assessment of Readiness for College and Careers [PARCC]. (2011). *PARCC model content frameworks: English language arts/literacy grades 3–11.* Retrieved from http://www.parcconline.org/sites/parcc/files/PARCCMCFELALiteracyAugust2012_FINAL.pdf

Pearson, P. D. (2004). The reading wars. *Educational Policy, 18*(1), 216–252.

Pearson, P.D. (2013). Research foundations of the Common Core State Standards in English language arts. In S. B. Neuman and L. B. Gambrell (Eds.), *Quality reading instruction in the age of common core standards* (pp. 237–262). Newark, DE: International Reading Association.

Pearson, P. D., & Gallagher, G. (1983). The gradual release of responsibility model of instruction. *Contemporary Educational Psychology, 8,* 112–123.

Petrilli, M. J., & Finn, C. E., Jr. (2010, October 10). Common core standards: What now? *Education Gadfly Weekly, 10*(39). Available: http://www.edexcellence.net/commentary/education-gadfly-weekly/2010/october-21/common-core-standards-now-what.html

Popham, W. J. (2008). *Transformative assessment.* Alexandria, VA: ASCD.

RAND Reading Study Group. (2002). Reading for understanding: Toward an R&D program in reading comprehension. Retrieved from http://www.rand.org/pubs/monograph_reports/MR1465.html

Ravitch, D. (2013, March 25). Should the common core standards have been field tested? [blog post]. Retrieved from http://dianeravitch.net/2013/03/25/should-the-common-core-standards-have-been-field-tested

Robb, L. (2002, May/June). The myth of learn to read/read to learn. *Scholastic Instructor, 111*(8), 23. Available: http://www.scholastic.com/teachers/article/myth-learn-readread-learn

Rosenblatt, L. M. (1978). *The reader, the text, the poem: The transactional theory of the literary work.* Carbondale, IL: Southern Illinois University Press.

Rosenblatt, L. M. (1995). *Literature as exploration* (5th ed.). New York: Modern Language Association.

Rylant, C. (2003). *The lighthouse family: The storm.* New York: Simon & Schuster Books for Young Readers.

Samuels, S. J. (2007). The DIBELS tests: Is speed of barking at print what we mean by reading fluency? *Reading Research Quarterly, 42,* 563–566.

Santa, C., & Havens, L. (1995). *Creating independence through student-owned strategies: Project CRISS.* Dubuque, IA: Kendall Hunt.

Savage, S. (2006). *Rainforest animals: Focus on habitats.* London: Hodder Weyland.

Shanahan, T. (2009, September 28). Putting students into books for instruction [blog post]. Retrieved from http://www.shanahanonliteracy.com/2009/09/putting-students-into-books-for.html

Shanahan, T. (2012, June 18). What is close reading? [blog post]. Retrieved from http://www.shanahanonliteracy.com/2012/06/what-is-close-reading.html

Shanahan, T. (2013, August 11). Text dependency is too low a standard [blog post]. Retrieved from http://www.shanahanonliteracy.com/2013/08/text-dependency-is-too-low-standard.html

Shanahan, T., & Shanahan, C. (2008, Spring). Teaching disciplinary literacy to adolescents: Rethinking content-area literacy. *Harvard Education Review, 78*(1), 40–59.

Shanahan, T., & Shanahan, C. (2012, January/March 2012). What is discipline literacy and why does it matter? *Topics in Language Disorders, 32*(1), 7–18.

Smith, M. W., Wilhelm, H. D., & Fredricksen, J. E. (2012). *Oh, yeah?! Putting argument to work both in school and out (exceeding Common Core standards).* Portsmouth, NH: Heinemann.

Snow, C. E. (n.d). *Improving reading outcomes: Getting beyond third grade.* Retrieved from http://www.gse.harvard.edu/~snow/Aspen_snow.html

Sotomayor, S. (2013). *My beloved world.* New York: Knopf.

Stenner, A. J., Koons, H., & Swartz, C. W. (2010). *Text complexity and developing expertise in reading.* Durham, NC: MetaMetrics, Inc.

Vygotsky, L. S. (1978). *Mind in society: The development of higher psychological processes.* Cambridge, MA: Harvard University Press.

Webb, N., et al. (2005, July 24). WAT: Web alignment tool. Wisconsin Center of Educational Research, University of Wisconsin-Madison. Retrieved from http://www.wcer.wisc.edu/WAT/index.aspx

Wessling, S. B., Lillge, D., & VanKooten, C. (2011). *Supporting students in a time of core standards: Grades 9–12.* Urbana, IL: National Council of Teachers of English.

Williamson, G. L. (2006). *Aligning the journey with a destination: A model for K–16 reading standards.* Durham, NC: MetaMetrics.

Wineburg, S. S. (1991). On the reading of historical texts: Notes on the breach between school and academy. *American Educational Research Journal, 28,* 495–519.

Wineburg, S. S. (1998). Reading Abraham Lincoln: An expert/expert study in the interpretation of historical texts. *Cognitive Science, 22,* 319–346.

Wurman, R. S. (2001). *Information anxiety 2.* Indianapolis, IN: Que.

Yopp, R. H., & Yopp, H. K. (2006). Informational texts as read-alouds at school and home. *Journal of Literacy Research, 38*(1), 37–51.

Zawilinski, L., & Leu, D. J. (2008, March 27). *A taxonomy of skills and strategies from verbal protocol of accomplished adolescent Internet users.* Paper presented at the American Educational Research Association Conference, New York, New York.

Zygouris-Coe, V. (2012). Disciplinary literacy and the Common Core State Standards. *Topics in Language Disorders, 32*(1), 35–50.

INDEX

The letter *f* following a page number denotes a figure.

ABOUT THE AUTHORS

Diane Lapp, EdD, is Distinguished Professor of Education in the Department of Teacher Education at San Diego State University (SDSU), where she teaches both preservice and graduate courses in literacy education. During her career, Diane has taught in elementary, middle, and high schools, and she has recently had the opportunity to return to the classroom to teach 6th grade English and Earth Science at Health Sciences Middle School in San Diego, where she is also an instructional coach at both the middle school and Health Sciences High and Middle College. Diane's major areas of research and instruction are issues related to struggling readers and writers, their families, and their teachers. Currently a coeditor of *Voices from the Middle*, published by National Council of Teachers of English, Diane has authored, coauthored, and edited numerous articles, columns, texts, handbooks, and children's materials on reading, language arts, and instructional issues, including the Common Core State Standards. She has also chaired and co-chaired several International Reading Association (IRA) and Literacy Research Association committees. A member of both the California and International Reading Halls of Fame, her many educational awards include being named as Outstanding Teacher Educator and Faculty Member in the Department of Teacher Education at SDSU, Distinguished Research Lecturer from SDSU's Graduate Division of Research, IRA's 1996 Outstanding Teacher Educator of the Year, and IRA's 2011 John Manning Award recipient for her work in public schools. Diane can be reached at lapp@mail.sdsu.edu. For additional information, please visit http://edweb.sdsu.edu/people/DLapp/DLapp.html.

Barbara Moss, Ph.D, is a professor of literacy education at San Diego State University, where she teachers both preservice and graduate courses in literacy education. During her long career in the public schools, she taught reading or English language arts at the elementary, middle, and high school levels. In addition, she worked as a reading specialist, a reading supervisor, and a high school literacy coach. She has worked as a university professor in both Ohio and California. Her research interests focus on children's literature in the classroom, especially informational texts, disciplinary literacy, and teacher implementation of instructional strategies. Barbara has published widely in literacy journals including *The Reading Teacher*, *The Journal of Literacy Research*, and *Reading and Writing Quarterly*. She regularly presents at professional conferences on a range of topics, including children's literature, close reading, and the Common Core State Standards. She has served as the editor of *The Ohio Reading Teacher* and on the editorial board of *The Reading Teacher* and several other literacy journals. She has served as a staff developer for numerous school districts and done hundreds of professional presentations for teachers across the country, both face to face and online. She has authored, co-authored, or edited numerous books on topics including independent reading, classroom strategies for teaching informational texts, new literacies, and children's nonfiction trade books. Her most recently co-authored books include *Thirty Five Strategies for Guiding Readers through Informational Texts* (Guilford Press) and *Not This But That: No More Independent Reading Without Support* (Heinemann). She also recently served as the Young Adult Literature column editor for *Voices in the Middle*, an NCTE publication. She can be reached at bmoss@mail.sdsu.edu.

Maria Grant, EdD, is an associate professor in secondary education at California State University, Fullerton (CSUF). She has authored numerous publications centered on close reading, Common Core State Standards, science literacy, formative assessment, and reading in the content areas, including articles in *Educational Leadership* and the *Journal of Adolescent & Adult Literacy*. Additionally, she is coauthor of *Reading and Writing in Science: Tools to Develop Disciplinary Literacy*, with Douglas Fisher, and *Teaching Students to Think Like Scientists: Strategies Aligned with Common Core and Next Generation Science Standards*, with Douglas Fisher and Diane Lapp. Her most recent work focuses on the Common Core State Standards for English Language Arts, concentrating on support for teachers working to implement the six shifts of ELA standards, move students toward reading more informational text, and use close reading in the classroom. Additionally, she works with teachers to implement key elements of the new Science Framework and the Next Generation Science Standards. Maria teaches courses in the credential and graduate programs at CSUF and conducts professional development with teachers at various schools across the country.

She is currently director of the Intern Program and leads the Literacy Summer Seminar Series at CSUF. Maria can be reached at mgrant@fullerton.edu.

Kelly Johnson, PhD, a National Board Certified teacher, is a Common Core Support Teacher in the San Diego Unified School District, where she works in classrooms with teachers, modeling how to implement the Common Core strategies across the disciplines and grades. A faculty member in teacher education at San Diego State University, Kelly teaches reading methods, classroom management, and liberal studies. She received the California Reading Association's Constance McCullough Research Award for her study on assessment and diagnostic instruction. Kelly also received the International Reading Association's Celebrate Literacy Award, which honors educators for their significant literacy contributions. Kelly has published in *The Reading Teacher, The California Reader, The Reading Professor,* and *Literacy.* She has also coauthored several books: *Accommodating Differences Among English Language Learners: 75+ Literacy Lessons (2nd and 3rd editions), Designing Responsive Curriculum: Planning Lessons That Work,* and *Teaching Literacy in First Grade (Tools for Teaching Literacy).* Often referred to by her colleagues as a teacher's teacher, Kelly has appeared in many instructional videos on teacher modeling, assessment and instruction, effective grouping, and writing instruction. Her current focus is assessment and small-group instruction in secondary classrooms. Prior to her current secondary and postsecondary positions, Kelly taught grades 1–6 and worked as a peer coach and a reading intervention teacher. She can be reached at kjohnson@hshmc.org.

RELATED ASCD RESOURCES

At the time of publication, the following ASCD resources were available (ASCD stock numbers appear in parentheses). For up-to-date information about ASCD resources, go to www.ascd.org.

ASCD EDge Group
Exchange ideas and connect with other educators interested in various topics, including "The Common Core in the Classroom," "English and Language Arts," and "Literacy, Language, Literature" on the social networking site ASCD EDge™ at http://edge.ascd.org/

Print Products
Common Core State Standards for Elementary Grades K–2 Math & English Language Arts: A Quick-Start Guide by Amber Evenson, Monette McIver, Susan Ryan, and Amitra Schwols; edited by John Kendall (#113014)

Common Core State Standards for Elementary Grades 3–5 Math & English Language Arts: A Quick-Start Guide by Amber Evenson, Monette McIver, Susan Ryan, and Amitra Schwols; edited by John Kendall (#113015)

Engaging Minds in English Language Arts Classrooms: The Surprising Power of Joy by Mary Jo Fresch; edited by Michael F. Opitz and Michael P. Ford (#113021)

The Multiple Intelligences of Reading and Writing: Making the Words Come Alive by Thomas Armstrong (#102280)

Teaching Reading in the Content Areas: If Not Me, Then Who? 3rd edition by Vicki Urqhart and Dana Frazee (#112024)

Total Literacy Techniques: Tools to Help Students Analyze Literature and Informational Texts by Pérsida Himmele and William Himmele, with Keely Potter (#114009)

PD Online
Common Core Literacy Foundations: Grades K–2 (#PD14OC002M)

Common Core Literacy: Grades 3–5 (#PD14OC007M)

Six Research-Based Literacy Strategies for the Elementary Classroom (#PD09OC24)

DVD
The Innovators: Integrating Literacy into Curriculum DVD (#613070)

The Whole Child Initiative helps schools and communities create learning environments that allow students to be healthy, safe, engaged, supported, and challenged. To learn more about other books and resources that relate to the whole child, visit www.wholechildeducation.org.

For more information: send e-mail to member@ascd.org; call 1-800-933-2723 or 703-578-9600, press 2; send a fax to 703-575-5400; or write to Information Services, ASCD, 1703 N. Beauregard St., Alexandria, VA 22311-1714 USA.